"These pages are brimming with wisdom, ideas, encouragement, and biblical guidance for parents wanting to raise their kids to thrive in mind, body, and spirit. Even before I had my own kids, I was inspired by Jodi's intentional approach to parenting and the beautiful family culture she was creating in her home. If you are in the early parenting years like me, this book is a hope-filled handbook full of relatable stories and struggles but also helpful solutions!"

Audrey Roloff, *New York Times* bestselling author of *A Love Letter Life* and cofounder of *The Marriage Journal*

"I have known and looked up to Jodi for more than ten years, and for ten years I have waited for her to write this book—finally! She could have kept all of this hard-won wisdom to herself, but that's never been who she is. In taking the time to write it all down and share it with all of us, Jodi has offered a generous gift to families everywhere for years to come."

Raechel Myers, mama of two and founder and CEO of She Reads Truth

"*The Whole and Healthy Family* is rich with practical and accessible ideas to help your family grow healthier physically, emotionally, and spiritually. Jodi's ideas are straightforward and full of thoughtful wisdom and insight. This book is not a list of things to do but rather an invitation to look deeper at the systems and structures of your family and see where you can grow. Best of all, it is an invitation to know your children in deep and intimate ways. I walked away from *The Whole and Healthy Family* feeling inspired and empowered to help my family flourish."

Greta Eskridge, author of *Adventuring Together* and *100 Days of Adventure*

"When I think of Jodi Mockabee—and by extension her book *The Whole and Healthy Family*—the word that comes to mind is *intentionality*. Jodi's dedication to not just coasting through her days as a parent but instead being intentional to both study what helps her family thrive and measure it against what Scripture has to say on the subject is both convicting and inspiring. I know this resource will benefit so many families who are looking for practical and conceptual ways to heal fractures within their own homes."

Abbie Halberstadt, author of *M Is for Mama*

"I've had the gift of walking alongside and witnessing Jodi during this season of being a wife and mother, and it has been a sharpening experience for me personally. *The Whole and Healthy Family* is a beautiful glimpse in written form into Jodi's home and the intentionality that has gone into every aspect of her family—mind, body, and soul. Brimming with wisdom, these pages are humbly filled with truths and practical tips I know will help shape families and homes for years to come."

Lynsey Kramer, wife, mother, and farmer at Yonder Way Farm

"Oh how I wish I had had this beautiful book at the beginning of my child-rearing journey. Jodi's humble offering is chock-full of insight and practical wisdom while always encouraging you to trust and listen to that still small voice in regards to your unique family and gifts. Jodi presents such great ideas to ponder, and she prods us to pray, think, and know our God and our children in order to parent well."

Terri Woods, homeschooling mama to nine and co-owner of Field + Forage

THE WHOLE
AND **HEALTHY**
FAMILY

THE WHOLE
AND HEALTHY
FAMILY

Helping Your Kids Thrive
in Mind, Body, and Spirit

JODI MOCKABEE

Revell

a division of Baker Publishing Group
Grand Rapids, Michigan

© 2022 by Jodi Mockabee

Published by Revell
a division of Baker Publishing Group
PO Box 6287, Grand Rapids, MI 49516-6287
www.revellbooks.com

Library of Congress Cataloging-in-Publication Data
Names: Mockabee, Jodi, 1980– author.
Title: The whole and healthy family : helping your kids thrive in mind, body, and spirit / Jodi Mockabee.
Description: Grand Rapids, MI : Revell, a division of Baker Publishing Group, [2022] | Includes bibliographical references.
Identifiers: LCCN 2021056552 | ISBN 9780800740139 (paperback) | ISBN 9780800742409 (casebound) | ISBN 9781493434350 (ebook)
Subjects: LCSH: Parenting—Religious aspects—Christianity. | Child rearing—Religious aspects—Christianity. | Families—Religious life.
Classification: LCC BV4529 .M58 2022 | DDC 248.8/45—dc23/eng/20220120
LC record available at https://lccn.loc.gov/2021056552

This publication is intended to provide helpful and informative material on the subjects addressed. Readers should consult their personal health professionals before adopting any of the suggestions in this book or drawing inferences from it. The author and publisher expressly disclaim responsibility for any adverse effects arising from the use or application of the information contained in this book.

Some names and details have been changed to protect the privacy of the individuals involved.

Published in association with The Bindery Agency, www.TheBinderyAgency.com.

Baker Publishing Group publications use paper produced from sustainable forestry practices and post-consumer waste whenever possible.

22 23 24 25 26 27 28   7 6 5 4 3 2 1

To my beloved husband, I am honored to be your wife.
Thank you for always laughing with me.
To my precious children,
I am humbled to have been chosen to be your mother
and love you more than words can express.
Thank you for being willing to share our story with others.
God is good!

CONTENTS

INTRODUCTION

What does it mean to have a whole family? The term *whole* doesn't mean perfected or finished but rather encompasses the idea of cultivating and stewarding the minds, bodies, and spirits of our children. We do so while they are in our home so that, in turn, they can raise whole families of their own. In Luke 10:27, Jesus charged his followers with a holistic approach to love by quoting Deuteronomy 6, saying, "You shall love the Lord your God with all your heart and with all your soul and with all your strength and with all your mind." He recognized that our beings are made of separate parts that must work together to create a whole person.

With this goal in mind, my husband and I have learned to nourish and equip our children in each area of their being. This book shares what we have learned, and it is not a "how-to" but a "how we" regarding family philosophy, ideals, and culture. Much of our whole family philosophy came from a place of hopelessness and exhaustion during those early years of parenting, which I like to refer to as "the trenches." Perhaps you are in the trenches now, with one or more babies in diapers, sleepless nights, and constant feedings. While our young children brought blessings and joy into our home, they also were so unique in their needs that it felt at times like we were grasping for respite as we tried to meet them all. During those years, my husband, Jason, and I found a comedy act from Jim Gaffigan that summed up the trenches perfectly. In discussing what it was like to have four children, Jim said, "Imagine you're drowning—and someone tosses you a baby!"[1] Regardless of how many children you have, parenting can certainly feel like drowning at times, but there are ways to thrive instead of merely survive.

A good portion of our family culture came as we created a home environment for our firstborn child, whom we eventually learned had special needs. Little did we know that some of the practices we put in place for him to prosper would also be beneficial to the rest of our children. Many of our practices grew out of problem-solving, and we learned to start praying about nearly every decision, big and small. How would the current choice before us fit within our family ideals of intention and wholeness? Soon enough we discovered that the smallest of decisions could affect the core of our family values. Day by day, intent became a big part of our decision-making process, and what we envisioned for our family culture became our measuring stick.

You'll find personal stories woven throughout this book to illustrate a belief or strategy, and most of them are about our children. Our children gave us permission to share their stories. Some stories may not mention names to protect the privacy of that specific child. Keep in mind that for every story in this book that shows the fruit of our parenting, there are probably a dozen more stories of failure and frustration. Jason and I do not have it all together, nor will we ever, as we are sinful human beings. We are still in our parenting years, as all of our children still live in our home.

The hope of this book is to help provide ideas and solutions that will shape the foundation of your parenting journey. Some information in this book is derived from data I have researched extensively, but please keep in mind that I am not a health coach or a doctor. Our health and medical choices have been a result of research, education, experience, prayer, and discernment. While I am happy to share any information I have learned, each family should spend time researching on their own, so they are confident in the path that they choose.

Not every idea or practice in our household will align with your own personal convictions; this book is not a guide or a standard but a reflection of what has worked in our home with our individual gifts, weaknesses, and personalities. We are raising our family based on our own relationship with God and his direction, and while we attempt to walk in obedience, there is always room for growth. I'm not writing as an authority figure but rather want to walk alongside you, sharing the tools that work for us and how we have come to create our family culture in hopes that you will find a nugget here and there to add to yours.

WHOLE MINDS

1

AWARENESS

There are three things extremely hard: steel, a diamond, and to know one's self.

Benjamin Franklin

Our job as parents is to assess and encourage the wholeness of our family and each individual person within our home, just as Paul approached the church in Corinth:

> Now there are varieties of gifts, but the same Spirit; and there are varieties of service, but the same Lord; and there are varieties of activities, but it is the same God who empowers them all in everyone. To each is given the manifestation of the Spirit for the common good. . . . As it is, there are many parts, yet one body. (1 Cor. 12:4–7, 20)

In the body of Christ, we see many working parts within the church. On a smaller scale, a family functions just the same. Each person was crafted to be a part of the family and has God-given gifts that should be recognized, cultivated, and used to go out and serve others.

Knowing Your Children

Early in my motherhood journey, I found the book *Discover Your Children's Gifts* by Don and Katie Fortune. I was elated to dive deeper into understanding who God created my children to be. That book helped me parent my children according to their individual personalities, needs, and gifts. The basis for the Fortunes' teaching is Romans 12:6–8:

> Having gifts that differ according to the grace given to us, let us use them: if prophecy, in proportion to our faith; if service, in our serving; the one who teaches, in his teaching; the one who exhorts, in his exhortation; the one who contributes, in generosity; the one who leads, with zeal; the one who does acts of mercy, with cheerfulness.

This was the first book I found about children's motivational gifts, and it taught me about different approaches for discipline and stewardship related to the varied gifts and personalities innate in our children. The most memorable part of the book for me was the chapter that began with, "The perceiver is, perhaps, the most challenging child to raise."[1] That described one of my children, and for the first time I felt heard! There are many positive characteristics of a perceiver, yet reading about some of the challenges made me feel less alone as a mother and more prepared for what our potential future looked like with this child. It painted a realistic picture for the complexity of a child who is sensitive and responsible yet has an iron will, and it gave practical counsel on how to handle certain situations. As I read through some of the parenting advice, I was able to look at it through the lens of parenting that specific child, not all of my children as a whole. The same goes for my other children, who possess their own motivational gifts. Paul's words started becoming evident in our family: many parts, one body.

It has been over ten years since I first read that book, and the information that resonated then is still applicable now. All children are born with special gifts and personalities. We can shape their characters and help steward their hearts, but the gifts and personalities they were born with will always remain the same. The earlier we recognize this, the more efficient and effective our parenting can be to help encourage our children in their strengths, stretch them in their weaknesses, and develop lasting, meaningful connections with them.

Learning how my children operate has helped me parent more efficiently. To use the term *efficient* in regard to relationships may sound a bit administrative, but to be honest, when you have five children, you will take efficiency in every form! One of my favorite unintentional parenting books is *Cheaper by the Dozen* by Frank Gilbreth Jr. It's a hilarious account of his childhood, being raised with eleven other siblings and by a father who was constantly on the quest for more efficiency. His father, Frank Sr., once said, "There is no waste in the world that equals the waste of needless, ill-directed, and inefficient motions."[2] You can buy all the toys in the world for a child, but if all they want is quality time from you, then those toys can translate as ill-directed love. I learned from our firstborn that I could absolutely be shooting in the dark in many areas such as discipline, affection, attention, and activities. Every child is so different, and learning about their motivations provides a targeted approach to building a healthy relationship with them.

Identifying your child's love language is a great way to help understand how your child gives and receives love. In Gary Chapman and Ross Campbell's book *The 5 Love Languages of Children*, you can discover the ways your children prefer to give and accept love. Chapman says, "Every child has a different way of perceiving love. There are five ways children (indeed, all people) speak and understand emotional love."[3] By identifying which type of expression of love your child likes to give or receive, your message to your child can be communicated much more efficiently, and you can recognize the ways in which they are showing love to you.

Our second son, Everett, receives love through touch. For him, touch doesn't just look like gentle affection. He needs serious sensory input, meaning a lot of physicality. Everett feels loved the most when we wrestle with him or give him a playful shove when he walks by. This took some getting used to for Jason, because he grew up with sisters and was never allowed to be aggressive with them. He has been realizing how much Everett loves good roughhousing. When we read aloud, Everett will fight to sit next to me. When I was teaching him how to read, I discovered he did much better when he was sitting on my lap. Touch is important for him to feel secure and loved, even if it looks like a playful punch on the arm. Each child is different in the way they show love and need love shown to them. Finding out how they tick and parenting with that in mind is another tool in developing a strong bond with them.

As your children grow, you will start recognizing consistent traits that stand out. Some of these traits will be beautiful and positive, and others will have negative tendencies. Naming such traits is a way to help your children understand who they are and how God created them. For example, my daughter, Scarlett, is very detail-oriented and likes to finish a task knowing she did the best job possible. While this is a wonderful trait, it can cripple her at times. We talk through what it's like to be detail-oriented, and we also talk about how that can translate to being a perfectionist. These same traits also cross over relationally, as she can be extremely attentive and loves to please but can struggle with self-condemnation when she knows she has done wrong. Walking through situations with your children and identifying these traits takes time, but it also provides them with the ability to name and recognize what they are feeling and experiencing. By doing so, they can learn to find joy and fulfillment in their gifts and tame their weaknesses.

Efficient Connections

There are several ways to speak to the heart of your child. Jason and I take notes on our children's favorite activities and desires. We use errands in town to create opportunities for alone time with each child. Some parents take their children on dates, but this is not an effective tool in our family because we have too many to keep track of. We just try to pay attention to who needs some special time and, depending on the child, will treat them to something they love while we are out. One of our children isn't as much into treats as he is into activities, so we'll take him on a quick hike or to discover a new place together. Another loves fishing, so we'll throw a pole in the car and make a stop by the river on the way to the grocery store. My daughter loves dogs, so we'll take our dog on our errand and stop at the dog park so she can check out all the other breeds. These little errands become personal investments into their love accounts, showing them we care about their needs and desires and like spending time with them.

Establishing multiple forms of communication is another way we connect with our kids. We set up email accounts for each of our children as soon as they learned to type. Jason and I will email them little notes of appreciation or affirmation. We tell them we are thinking of them or include links to information we think they may enjoy. Some children appreciate these messages more than others. My youngest son, Elias, checks his email once a day and not only emails us but his grandparents as well. It makes him feel connected and loved. Emails have also become a way for my children to express concern or ask difficult questions. It opens a different avenue for children to communicate. Writing letters can be used the same way.

One day I got an email from my thirteen-year-old stating he was concerned about college. He didn't understand how all of the units worked and wanted to know his educational plan so that he could prepare for it. I had to laugh and enjoy the moment, because, in bullet-point fashion, he managed to clearly communicate his concerns about a topic that meant a lot to him. Writing that email probably allowed him to organize his thoughts much more than a conversation would have. Little did he know that I had no idea what his educational plan would entail. At that time, all I could do was plan our homeschool a week in advance! It did, however, motivate me to think more long-term about his future as I realized how important it was to him.

Recently I received an email from Scarlett. She had been mourning the death of her sweet lapdog, Della, for several months, and was campaigning to adopt another dog. She wrote a persuasive email, including links for training plans, costs of care, and breed information to prove she could care for another pet. Being the pushovers we are when it comes to our children's hearts, she ended up getting another lapdog. Jason and I both recognized that when Della died, Scarlett lost an opportunity to exercise her gifts of nurturing and compassion, but to be honest, that impressive email is what drove our decision! We continue to use email as one form of communication, and I pray it will remain a way for us to stay in touch with our children in a meaningful way during future days when we can't always have a conversation face-to-face.

Some of our friends whose children have phones will send them life-giving texts filled with Scripture and encouragement, as well as fun banter and selfies. Other friends will put notes for their children in their school lunch bags. Going above and beyond the typical parental "duties" to show love for children provides an extra level of attachment, which opens the door for accountability as well.

When I began homeschooling, I dove into researching many educational pedagogies and was enamored with many of the ideas and strategies for ensuring that my children would receive the best education. One day I discovered the philosophy of unschooling and was instantly intrigued. Unschooling encompasses the belief that children do not really earn an education unless they own it personally. For this to happen, the desire to learn has to come from within them, meaning they need to seek out information and knowledge on their own terms and apply them in real life. Through this philosophy, a parent is just present to help guide them and support them in their journey, not to lay it out before them. While we didn't fully adopt unschooling in our home education model, I loved the idea of becoming not only a partner with but also a student of my children. I realized that this idea does not just apply to education but to parenting as well.

Getting to know the depths of your child's heart only comes by spending time with that child and observing the behaviors and motivations with which they respond to life's experiences. Intentionally partnering with and studying the gifts and characteristics that God put within your child will allow you to connect with them in an effective and impactful way. Keeping that connection will build a fruitful relationship that creates room for accountability and direction in their lives as they make daily decisions that will shape their character. This is why we have chosen to be efficient in our connection with our children because we are building a trustworthy relationship in which we can train them up in the way they should go (Prov. 22:6).

Knowing Ourselves

I never knew I struggled with anger until I became the parent of a challenging child. The boiling reaction in my chest kept surprising me, as I had never been the angry type. Becoming a parent can certainly awaken some of your deepest, darkest weaknesses, and sometimes I think that certain children are sent to sanctify us as parents. It wasn't until a neighbor mentioned my anger that I realized how freely I had relied on yelling. We were living in a rental in a tight-squeezed neighborhood. I was home with three children, and Jason was commuting to work hours away, only coming home on the weekends. I was frazzled and had not been putting much time into the Word of God or my character. One day, as we were running through the neighborhood, a neighbor came out to officially meet us. I introduced her to my children, and by the time I had made it to Carter, she asked, "Let me guess, this is Carter?" I was dumbfounded. She chuckled and then followed up with, "Well, I've heard you yell his name often enough." Ouch. It was one of those moments that hit me in the gut. I knew I had been struggling with anger, but I didn't realize that I had gotten so out of control that a neighbor had to subtly call me out on it!

The good news is that God is a forgiving God. He is merciful and slow to anger (Ps. 86:15), two character traits that sometimes feel nearly impossible to practice in parenting. The neighbor's comment was exactly what I needed to assess what had happened to my character. Why had I lost control so easily, and how did I get to that point? Shortly after that experience, I picked up a personality book and took its quizzes. I don't even remember which one it was, but I do remember scoring incredibly low in the compassion category. I didn't know it at the time, but my challenging child was experiencing struggles of his own, many of which were a result of him being neurologically atypical. My lack of compassion mixed with his high needs made space for a short temper and a quick tongue. Since that day I have asked for forgiveness time and time again for the way I handled many situations with him. It's humbling to look back at some of the times I'd yelled, knowing that I hadn't been the parent he needed me to be. Thankfully he has forgiven me, and continues to do so whenever I fail.

Discovering some of my weaknesses allowed me to forecast situations that could cause me to lose my patience or allow an angry outburst. Once I knew what triggered these behaviors, I was able to prepare for the situation in advance and have a plan. Whenever I made it peacefully through a situation, I could go home, put the kids down for their nap, and reward myself with a cup of coffee and something sweet. If I was not successful, I'd go home and try to identify the moment where I lost control. When I would ask forgiveness of my children, I would often tell them what I had done wrong and what I should have done to defuse the situation. I wanted them to know that I was aware of my struggle with yelling, because confessing my sin provided me with a way to be held accountable.

Asking for forgiveness has become a habit in our parenting (although Jason seems to not have to ask as much as I do!), because we are not perfect parents. Also, by asking for forgiveness, we are modeling what it looks like to own up to our mistakes. Ephesians 4:32 says, "Be kind to one another, tenderhearted, forgiving one another, as God in Christ forgave you." We have seen the fruit of this practice, as now our older children will ask us for forgiveness without prompting when they have acted out. We still have to walk our younger children through this when conflict arises. When we have these conversations, we always try to end them on a light note, making fun of ourselves or letting our children tease us as long as it's not disrespectful. We want them to learn and know that reconciliation is not to be feared or avoided but can be a beautiful process and have a healthy outcome.

Even though I still struggle with anger, I have been able to learn some techniques that have helped me gain control of my emotions. One of my mentors and friends taught me the phrase, "Slow is fast." This phrase applies specifically to my neurodiverse child, who functions best with full explanations and descriptions of what I'd like him to do or why he can't do something. This took years for me to learn, as I tend to be very direct and like to move from task to task quickly. Now, when I can tell he needs a full explanation, I remind myself that "slow is fast," and it helps me realize that I can spend a few extra minutes in the moment to sit down and discuss—or I can cause a full-blown meltdown that will result in an hour of heated emotions on both sides.

When I get angry while I am in the house, I have learned to do something physical and productive, as sometimes that combination blows off steam. I will sweep the kitchen or reorganize the pantry to logically step myself through a calming process. I have practiced this technique so many times that if the children see a broom in my hand, they know I might be working through some things. It's an ongoing joke not to mess with Mom when she has the broom!

I am still on a journey of getting to know who I am as an individual: why I tend to make certain decisions, why I react a specific way, and, most importantly, how to alter some of those behaviors. Some may call it self-discovery, but I think there can be a fine balance to understanding who you are in order to parent the way that God intends. Ephesians 6:4 says, "Fathers, do not provoke your children to anger, but bring them up in the discipline and instruction of the Lord." I want to be healthy and whole in the Lord so that I do not provoke my children or teach them unhealthy behaviors or habits from my own actions.

Knowing Your Spouse

If we look at the family unit as a miniature version of the church, we are reminded again of Paul's teaching about being made of many parts in one body. We discuss this concept specifically

FOR FURTHER READING

While Jason and I have read some marriage books together, we have found that books that help bring more awareness to our personality differences are more efficient in our marriage. Some of the books we have read are:

The Four Tendencies by Gretchen Rubin

Discovering Your Heart with the Flag Page by Mark Gungor

The Road Back to You by Ian Morgan Cron

The 5 Love Languages by Gary Chapman

whenever there are personality clashes or sibling quarrels. We would not be able to function as a family if everyone had the same role, nor would it be enjoyable. Marriage is very much the same, and Jason and I constantly remind ourselves that in our own family unit, in some situations one of us may be the heart and the other the head, but in other situations that may be reversed. If you are a single parent, you are probably acting as the head and the heart, which I can imagine would be a large and difficult role. Bless you and your leadership in your family!

Marriage is one of the most powerful ways we can glorify God, which is why I think it's also one of the hardest gifts to steward. Ephesians 5 gives us direct instructions on how to walk in love as believers and as husbands and wives. Husbands are to serve their wives by leading them and loving them with a sacrificial love (vv. 25–33), and wives are to serve their husbands by submitting to their leadership (vv. 22–24). When the husband and wife are both serving each other as God has intended, the marriage should reflect the glory of God, as a pure example of Christ and the church. However, that is a lot easier said than done.

Jason and I have found that it is a lot less difficult to serve one another when we understand each other's personal motivations. It took us quite a few years to realize that we are different people with different gifts and needs. It did not take us long, however, to notice each other's weaknesses! Once we were able to learn more about what motivated each other, we were able to adjust our expectations.

When you start to understand your spouse's gifts and tendencies, you tend to become an advocate for them. By doing so, you create a conversation the whole family can participate in and learn from. Jason recently sent me away for the weekend to jump-start the writing for this book. He sat the kids down and explained to them what the plan was. He told them that, in order for me to focus, I needed to be away from all distractions, and they worked together to create a plan so the house would be in order when I returned. It meant so much to me that he knew me well enough to do that. A few years ago, we went through a season that was incredibly draining for us all, but Jason especially. Every year we reserve a little cabin at a pack station in the high country for the family to stay for a week, but that year we decided to skip our family vacation and send Jason up there by himself to recharge. He really struggled with going alone, but we all knew he needed quiet time in the Word and in prayer. He had a wonderful time with the Lord and came back so refreshed. He thanked the kids and me for giving up our time in order to serve him. Letting your children be part of the process of support and compassion will allow them to understand the biblical model of serving one another in love.

There have been two motivations Jason and I have learned to accept and support in each other throughout the years, albeit they are complete opposites! We realized through reading *Discovering Your Heart with the Flag Page* that Jason is highly motivated by peace and I am motivated by achievement. One Christmas, shortly after we had finished going through the book, we found ourselves alone, which was unusual for a holiday. After a delicious breakfast feast and the opening of stocking stuffers, Jason stretched out on the couch for a mid-day snooze while I went to pull the power tools out of storage to finish a project in the twins' nursery. As I was nailing up pieces of tongue and groove, I laughed to myself about how much we were working within our motivations. Jason was resting in peace, and I was achieving my vision. We were able to talk about it later that afternoon and joke about the timing of reading that book, because I think if we weren't aware of our motivations, Jason would have been upset that I was working on something and probably would've felt guilty for not assisting, and I would've been frustrated that he wasn't helping me or making better use of a day off. Instead, we chose to give each other the best Christmas present ever: the ability to indulge in our internal motivations. We've had hundreds of similar situations since, in which we discuss each other's expectations to meet each other's needs. This isn't to say that every conversation is gently communicated, nor is it to say that we never have to compromise. Marriage is filled with compromising and serving, but it's a lot easier to do so when you know who you are working with and how to efficiently meet their needs and desires.

2

COMMUNICATION

Communication works for those who work at it.

John Powell

When Jason and I were dating, there was a moment in the car when I was giving him the silent treatment (I can't even remember what I was mad about; obviously it wasn't important). He asked me if I was upset. Because I was young and immature, I responded that I wasn't and continued to stare out the window. Moments later, he said, "Okay, here's the deal. If you're telling me you're not upset, I can only trust that what you're saying is true, so you can't blame me for anything I've done if you won't communicate about it. If you are upset, I think it's fair to give you a few minutes to explain what you are upset about. But if you don't start explaining within the next five minutes, you don't have the right to be angry." This completely took me by surprise. He was so forward yet so logical about it. I had two choices.

I could be ridiculous and avoid communicating my feelings, with nothing to gain, or I could share my thoughts and hope to resolve the issue with him. There were no other options. He gained my respect immediately, and I was able to lay out for him what I was thinking. The most fascinating part of this story is that, by nature, Jason is not forceful or demanding. I think God was really working through him for the sake of our relationship!

Ever since that moment, Jason and I have had a more open and healthier relationship in regard to communication and conflict resolution. That doesn't mean our marriage has been easy or without trials, but we did establish open communication early on in our relationship, which has helped in warding off bitterness while also encouraging accountability. When a couple commits to working through struggles and conflict with loving and clear communication, they teach their children to do the same.

Conflict Resolution

Jason's parents paid for us to go to premarital counseling when we were engaged. I don't remember much from it, but I do remember a few tips about conflict resolution that we both still practice today. I am so grateful for that gift, because these tips have helped diffuse a lot of emotional situations in our home.

1. Affirm your spouse or child before bringing up the subject matter. For example: "Everett, I love how adventurous and curious you are, but when we are doing school, you have to practice some self-control by finishing your work before going outside."
2. Mirror the feelings so your spouse or child feels heard and understood. "Let me see if I understand. You feel

disrespected because I made a joke about you in front of our friends, is that correct?" Sometimes mirroring the way your spouse or child feels allows you to understand the severity of the offense.

3. Try to find the root of the problem. Often the argument between you and your spouse or between siblings is not what the disagreement is really about. There's usually a root cause. We've had to work through a lot more of these discussions as our children have become teens with emotions that run higher and are more complex. In these situations, time and patience are needed, as it's almost like peeling an onion, trying to get to the middle. Each person should be able to deconstruct the situation by expressing what motivated their actions. You can guide your children through the situation, as you are creating a foundation for them to work through conflict with their future spouses and children. Not every spat requires intervention, but I have found that talking through offenses often heals open wounds that would otherwise continue to increase in size.

Conflict in Front of Children

I was raised in a home where I never observed any form of conflict between my parents. We only knew there was conflict when there was a suggestion that they discuss such matters in the bedroom. They never argued in front of us. (Later we learned that "discussing it in the bedroom" also meant other things!) I am grateful for such a peaceful childhood, as I never experienced much tension between my parents. However, I entered marriage with the grand idea that there should never be hard conversations. I was in for a rude awakening and, to be honest, I still struggle with discussing difficult things.

Notre Dame University psychologist E. Mark Cummings says,

> Conflict is a normal part of everyday experience, so it's not whether parents fight that is important, it's how the conflict is expressed and resolved, and especially how it makes children feel, that has important consequences for children. Watching some kinds of conflicts can even be good for kids—when children see their parents resolve difficult problems, they can grow up better off.[1]

There are many topics and discussions that Jason and I will save for the bedroom or another private place, as the content may not be appropriate for the children, but when we have a simple disagreement that involves just the two of us, we tend to communicate openly in front of our children, using the same practices of conflict resolution we were taught in premarital counseling. Modeling marital discussions is an excellent way to teach your children healthy communication skills. We try to keep our sense of humor intact and typically end with laughter, even if our children experienced a bit of tension. When we resolve an issue in front of them, Jason will often say something very positive about me (and sometimes vice versa) to the children, and we usually hug or kiss. They always have the biggest smirks and smiles after that.

Name It and Tame It

Just as Jason and I laid out our rules of communication in our early days of dating, we use the same tactic with our children.

There are a lot of books out there about the importance of letting children feel big feelings and big emotions. Both are important to a degree, but our feelings and emotions are fleeting. Many times, feelings and emotions that are not controlled can lead to self-destructive habits such as low self-esteem, procrastination, depression, and entitlement. Proverbs 25:28 says, "A man without self-control is like a city broken into and left without walls." Parents can teach children to identify emotions and feelings, understand their root cause, and find the right place for them. Often I will use the phrase, "Let's name it and tame it" to help them identify that something is out of control.

Psychological studies across the board have discovered that simple recognition of trauma can often be the largest step toward healing. Many times, traumatic situations or experiences that happen are never verbalized or explained to a child. This unresolved trauma can often turn into behavioral problems and/or health issues later in life. However, the same studies have shown that healing begins when the trauma is recognized, and with practice, the trauma can be denied a foothold on behavior or health. In other words, it's named and tamed. We teach our children to take big emotions and feelings, name them, understand their cause, and set them aside for the sake of self-control so they can learn how to move forward with life's disappointments and trials (even if they're not traumatic but just upsetting).

I'll give you a simple example. During a soccer tournament, one of my sons was matched up with a very physical and mouthy opponent. He kept leaning against my son, poking him intentionally, and saying crude and offensive things. That particular son has a strong sense of justice, and his anger was rising by the minute. After the game, he was so angry, he was shaking (it didn't help that they lost). I gave him a minute to calm down, and then we walked through our exercise. "Son, I can see you are angry," I said. He replied, "Yes, that kid was so rude, Mom. He was cussing and pushing me around for no reason! I feel like I want to punch him!" I replied, "Oh yes, I saw that, and I can tell that you have had enough. It's a valid reason to be angry, but sitting in that anger will only encourage your feelings of wanting to punch him. Take a walk, take deep breaths, and then you need to name it and tame it." All he needed was for someone to recognize the injustice of the other boy's behavior.

Our overall goal is for our children to be able to recognize the feeling or emotion themselves, put a name to it, and then put it to rest. By teaching them this little habit, we are giving them tools to build self-control and protect themselves from unresolved trauma or feelings that may later affect them physically or behaviorally.

With permission from my son Carter, I'd like to share an example of how naming and taming works with special needs children. Carter struggles with sensory processing. There was a year I decided it would be best for him to attend a few enrichment classes at a local homeschooling co-op. It was a difficult transition for him because of all the stimulation in the classroom. Normally when he would get overstimulated, it would result in an outburst that lasted hours, many times with no resolution. But as he got older, we were able to start naming the reason for his big feelings and reactions.

One day I asked him to name all of the forms of stimulation he experienced in one class. He proceeded to tell me that he could hear another student's jaw pop when he chewed gum. He could hear the wind whistling in the leaves of the trees outside. He could feel the vibration of the table from a student who was lightly tapping it with his fingers, and he could smell someone microwaving their lunch way down the hall while also smelling the bleach they used to mop the halls with. He named all of what he was taking in while his teacher was lecturing. He explained that it took so much energy to focus through all of the distractions that he was completely exhausted when he came home. But an amazing thing happened. Every time he named a struggle, he was able to put it aside. In the following weeks, he began to learn to ignore the noises and tame the anxiety that they caused.

This process did not happen overnight. It took years of both of us practicing this habit. When he was young, I had to name the things for him as I observed what triggered him. I would say, "I know these socks make your toes feel funny, and that doesn't change the fact that you need to keep your feet warm," or "Yes, this building is very loud and has many people, but we still need to be here." Eventually it became his load to bear, and thankfully he is equipped with the tools to make that load much lighter than it would otherwise be.

Creating a Healthy Sexual Culture within the Home

One of my favorite subjects to talk about with other parents is the sexual culture within the home, mostly because it is rarely talked about yet parents yearn for answers and discussion on this matter. As I grew up, the topic of sex was quite taboo, and there was an incredible amount of shame around it. I'm not sure if this was due to my experience being raised in the church and attending Christian schools, but I have found that many other parents relate to the same issue and have carried that shame into their adult lives and marriages.

Sex is everywhere. It's on billboards, it's rampant on the internet, and it's extremely accessible for even the youngest of children. But it's not talked about in the home. This causes a great disconnect for a child, developmentally and spiritually, especially if they are taught from a young age through church, parents, or friends that sex is wrong. How can something they're taught is so wrong be so accessible and advertised as right and normal? As a society, we have failed our children in this matter, but the good news is that, as parents, we have the ability to start our children on a healthy path to understanding their bodies, sex, and their responsibility to protect their minds from the overflow of sexual information and exposure.

A healthy sexual culture in the home begins with the absence of shame in naming body parts. Most households have certain names for biological body parts, such as "wee-wee" for the penis or "girly parts" for the vagina and urethra. If you call those body parts a nickname, ask yourself why. Likely it is because you are ashamed to call it what it is—which then places that shame upon your children, without them knowing or considering why. That's okay; that is a part of the learning process, and we are to recognize it first and then correct it to build a better sexual foundation for our children.

As soon as your son or daughter starts recognizing their genitalia, get in the practice of using the scientific name, just as you would call a nose a nose and a shoulder a shoulder. They should know that God made all parts for a purpose, and that they are whole in his image. This does not mean you do not teach them to protect their private parts. From as young as two years old, you can encourage them that their private areas are not for others to touch. We used the book *I Said NO* by Kimberly King from an early age to teach our children that their body is sacred and that private parts are private for a reason. When Jason and I went through rigorous sexual abuse training in our church, as was required for those in leadership positions, we learned that 90 percent of predators will stop their attempt to molest a child if the child says no. Teaching them to be confident in this response is imperative to protecting them when you are not around. Children who are confident in their bodies and their understanding of privacy, without shame, are less likely to be targets for predators.

Talking about private parts and privacy should not be a one-time discussion. The more you discuss body parts openly (without shame or condemnation), the more confident your child will be. I have had many parents throughout the years bring up the issue of masturbation in young children. Anyone who has had small children has probably seen it at one time or another. There are many nerve endings in both the penis and vagina, and children can feel those when they are exploring their own bodies. It's a tricky subject because you don't want to make them feel shameful by correcting them. You must note that there is nothing sexual about it for them. You're taking your adult understanding of sex and applying it to an innocent, curious child.

In our household, if I saw a child exploring or rocking, I would simply distract them and move them on to another task. If it was repetitive behavior, I would privately take them to another room and explain that I know it feels good, but because it's a private part, touching a private part in public (or in front of anyone) can be inappropriate. This is usually a developmental discovery, and they typically grow out of it (until adolescence, but that's a separate subject). By all means, try to avoid making fun, shaming, or calling your child gross, even though it makes you uncomfortable. Anytime you are openly communicating about body parts and sexual topics, you are establishing a healthy culture in your home, where your child can trust you not to shame them should they ever need to talk about sexual issues with you.

Many people have asked me, "At what age do you give the sex talk?" Let me introduce you to a doctrinal principle called the law of first mention. Theologian R. T. Kendall explains, "Law of first mention is a time-honoured hermeneutical method stating that the way a word is first used in the Bible will be the way this word is largely understood thereafter."[2] Your child's view of sex works no differently. Wherever or whoever they get their first description or picture of sex from will be the foundation that molds their idea of it.

Studies show that the average age of pornography exposure is now only eight years old. That is the average, meaning that children even younger are receiving their first lesson of sex from the internet or from friends with internet access. Instead of that first sex lesson being a biblical, trustworthy, and logical description of sex, they are getting a perverted and warped version of it that plants seeds of shame and confusion. This is why we should be the first to teach them about God's beautiful design for intimacy and creating a family. If their foundation and understanding of sex comes from open, informative conversations, from then on any sexual exposure (and there will be plenty) will be measured according to this information. Everything else will stand out as an altered view of God's design or your own foundational principles and will be easily recognizable.

To apply the law of first mention, you need to start talking about sex with your children from a young age. With our first two, we read the God's Design for Sex series, by Stan and Brenna Jones, starting around age five. With our last three, sex had become a common topic so we never needed to introduce the idea but just answered questions (and reading the Old Testament together definitely opens the door to many questions).

From observation with my own children, I can say they were not quite developmentally ready to understand the actual mechanics of sexual intercourse until about seven or eight years of age. Even though *sex* was a common word in our home, none of my children fully grasped its meaning until around that age.

Another common question people have asked me related to early conversations about sex is whether or not such conversations can awaken sexual feelings in a child prematurely. Children raised in openly communicative households are less likely to have sex in their teens and less apt to struggle with pornography addiction. However, if children are exposed to sexual content before they are developmentally able to process it, there is opportunity for great harm to be done psychologically.[3]

Now more than ever, online pornography is damaging our children's view of sex and sexuality. Dr. Cooper, a forensic pediatrician and staff member at the University of North Carolina School of Medicine, states that "Pornography normalizes sexual harm by portraying a lack of emotional relationship between consensual partners, unprotected sexual contact, and, in some instances, violence and rape."[4] In 2016 it was reported that 42 percent of children exposed to pornography sought out more aggressive forms of pornography. Dr. Cooper also states children are more vulnerable to the effects of pornography than adults because they have mirror neurons in their brain. Mirror neurons are important for development, as children learn through imitation.[5]

Several years ago, when we were a smaller family with two young toddlers, a family member was brave enough to share his story with us. He has given permission for me to share it here in hopes that parents will be more aware of the dangers of pornography. When he was about nine years old, he went over to a friend's house. His parents were there with him at the home, and the family was a trustworthy, Christian family. When the boys were all in the bedroom playing, his friend's brother brought him to a computer and showed him pornography, then pressured this young boy to act out what they had watched. This all happened while the families were visiting together in the kitchen. Our family member had never been taught about sex at this point, and had never been exposed to pornography, so you can imagine how confusing and shame-filled he must have felt at such a young age.

He blocked that memory out, but the trauma of that situation eventually started causing major behavioral and mental issues. When he went through puberty, he started experiencing extreme anger, depression, and anxiety, and when he was twenty-one, he decided to take his own life. Thankfully, somebody found him, and he chose to go through a recovery process. During that time in rehab, he was able to uncover the traumatic memory for the first time, and he was brave enough to share it with us young parents. His story has dramatically shaped my view of sex and pornography. If he was exposed at a trusted family's home, surely my children could be as well.

Because of the vast amount of technology available, I hope you understand that it is not a matter of if your children will be exposed to pornography; it's a matter of when. Our job as parents is to equip them to be able to cognitively handle the time when it comes.

Starting when your child is three years old, you can be gently teaching them how to report exposure to porn. *Good Pictures Bad Pictures* by Kristen A. Jenson gives a method for children to react when being exposed. It also walks them through the scientific process of what pornography does to the brain. Jenson breaks it down into simple language, stating that there are three parts to the brain: the thinking brain, the feeling brain, and the attraction center. When the attraction center is activated before the thinking brain (an understanding of sex), it can become imbalanced and cause anger, depression, sexual identity confusion, and more. Jenson also teaches children to have a plan when exposed to pornography. The child is to divert his or her eyes, call it what it is, tell an adult, and immediately start thinking of something different. In other words, they're to name and tame the situation.[6]

We have had great success with this plan. In fact, almost immediately after we read this book, we left town for a weekend away. On the way to our destination are some hot springs that we make a point to visit whenever we pass by. These hot springs are hidden under a little cliff we have to hike down to get to. Everett, who was seven at the time, was the first to get there. Within moments, he came running back up the hill, yelling, "Pornography, pornography!" Apparently the hot springs were already occupied. He had diverted his eyes and was in the process of calling it what it was while simultaneously letting an adult know! Since then there have been other situations we have been able to talk through and discuss—because I'd like to remind you that it is not a matter of if but when, and it's important that our children feel safe enough to talk about it.

I understand that a lot of this information may feel overwhelming, but there is good news. When your children are aware of the danger, they will want to protect themselves. With a few simple guidelines, you can set some basic boundaries in your home and with friends in order to help them succeed. Here are some of the boundaries we have put in place to limit our children's amount of exposure:

- No personal devices. We currently have two teen-agers, and they do not have cell phones with internet access nor do they have the ability to text or receive images. Because we have had so much discussion over the danger of pornography as well as addiction to phone usage, our teens are surprisingly okay with this arrangement.
- Computers and TVs are only in public places in the home, such as the kitchen table or living room. My children are allowed to use the computer, and they must have permission and a description of what they need it for, such as researching information or emailing their grandparents. We also look at the browser history and check in with them on whether they have witnessed anything inappropriate lately.
- We practice an open-door policy in our own home and in friends' homes. While we don't have devices in bed-rooms, we can't always control what our friends do, so our children know that they are to keep the doors open at all times. This also lowers the risk for peer-to-peer mo-lestation/experimental situations that commonly happen.

While creating a healthy sexual culture within the home is important to protect children from sexual abuse and pornography addiction, it also helps equip children to be able to handle the sexual temptations of their teen years and into adulthood. Your teen will have a sex drive, and it is important to accept that and not be in denial. Our bodies were created to start reproducing around age fourteen or fifteen, so to expect a teenager to not experience the sexual urges and feelings that come at that age is unrealistic. These sexual feelings do not make your teen dirty or sinful. They make them normal and designed to have a family. Your teen should not be shamed and should be recognized as a sexual human being. As a parent, it's your job to encourage them during a time that is extremely difficult to navigate.

We can also equip them to have a plan to manage their sex drive, which sticks with them through marriage, so when they're faced with temptation or have an open door toward infidelity, they are disciplined and have a plan in place to protect themselves, their spouse, and their family.

Setting up open communication, giving your child a plan for when they are tempted or exposed, and maintaining a healthy level of accountability will prepare the way for them to implement such disciplines in their adult life. Hopefully they will do the same with their children. My dream is to see my grandchildren's generation educated, equipped, and driven to practice a healthy sexual culture in their homes. Can you imagine what that would do to the porn industry and divorce rates?

3

NATURE

Let them once get in touch with nature and a habit is formed
which will be a source of delight and habit through life.

Charlotte Mason

I grew up on acreage with trees to climb, animals to tend, and
space to roam. Many times I could have been found lost in my
thoughts, perched on a branch of a pine tree, or hiking along
our creek. When I think about the stressful times of my life,
such as my father dying, putting myself through college, or
facing cancer, I recognize that I've always run to nature (often
literally) to help process the stress. In fact, I still run to nature
to process, and my hope is that my children will as well. Nature
plays a large role in our mental well-being.

Nature as an Outlet

Often you will hear the word *decompress* associated with activities such as playing video games, watching TV, and scrolling

through social media. As parents, we have the opportunity to introduce different methods of decompressing or coping to our children. We cannot protect them from a life filled with pain or sorrow, nor can we prevent them from making mistakes and suffering the consequences. But we can help them develop mentally by providing them with skills to navigate their way through tragedy or stress.

My goal for my children is that they turn to nature. Nature improves mental health. By our example and by inviting them into physical activities grounded in nature, we can help instill in them a better and healthier way to decompress.

Many different studies have shown that those who spend time in nature, compared to those who spend most of their time indoors, experience reduced levels of cortisol, which is a hormone that is often used as a marker for stress. There has also been research into how being in nature can decrease sympathetic nervous activity, systolic blood pressure, and even heart rate. For example, in one study that estimated the amount of time American people spend in transit, outdoors, and indoors, Stanford professor Wayne Ott concluded that "employed persons in the US spend only about 2% of their time outdoors, 6% of their time in transit, and 92% of their time indoors."[1] This could be one of the reasons that we, as a nation, are experiencing higher levels of stress, depression, suicide, and mental health issues. One of the solutions to such problems is simplistic and inexpensive: spend more time outdoors and in nature.

In 1982, the Japanese Ministry of Agriculture, Forestry, and Fisheries organized a grassroots wellness activity called *shinrin-yoku*, translated as "forest bathing." They realized that a natural environment can play a large role in mental health and established *shinrin-yoku* as a protocol in public health. The purpose of *shinrin-yoku* is not to exercise physically but to simply be in nature by connecting through the senses of sight, hearing, taste, smell, and touch. Other nations started adopting the same type of program, understanding the benefits nature can bring to a community.[2]

While I am grateful for studies and research that explore the benefits of nature, I am also concerned that we need the government to step in and suggest such therapy. Nature was created for our enjoyment, our provision, our health, and also as a reminder of God's mighty power and beauty. Nature should be a reason to praise our maker! Psalm 96:11–12 says, "Let the heavens be glad, and let the earth rejoice; let the sea roar, and all that fills it; let the field exult, and everything in it! Then shall all the trees of the forest sing for joy." Nature reminds us to be grateful and to give glory where glory is due.

Recently one of our twins, Elias, experienced a run-in between his finger and a large heavy door. The door split his finger open, and it was apparent that an ER trip was needed. He had never been to the ER and had spent very little time in a doctor's office, so he was a little bit nervous over what to expect. As we waited to be seen, I shared my strategy to help with pain management. First, I asked him where his favorite place in nature was (many times when we are outside, I'll ask the kids to take a picture of the scenery in their minds, as well as using their senses, so they can revisit it in the future). He described a ski run in Utah that looked over the entire city and ranges and ranges of mountains. It had been a windy afternoon, and he could feel the wind on his cheeks. He said it smelled like water, and he remembered feeling very warm except for his face. He remembered how light and fluffy the snow was and how it would just fall out of his gloves when he picked it up (he did not describe all of this on his own without prompting; I did need to ask him what it tasted like or what it felt like). After we talked through the scene and what his senses had noticed, I told him when it came time for the numbing shot and anything else that could cause fear or pain, to close his eyes, take deep, slow breaths, and remember that ski run in Utah. To smell the air, feel the wind, and embrace the warmth. And while doing that, he could pretend to be alone on that mountain with Jesus providing him comfort. "Tell him you love him and pray for strength and peace. Ask him questions and let him care for you," I said. "Think of your favorite Scripture verse and repeat it over and over until the procedure is over."

This mental and spiritual practice has walked me through three surgeries and other painful experiences. I have been able to share it with all of my children as a way to cope and handle tough situations with peace. Nature is a gift that keeps giving, even when you can't be outdoors and are stuck in an emergency room.

Before you consider nature as an outlet, it needs to be a part of your foundation. Typically, in stress, one flees to something safe and familiar, just as Elias did in the emergency room. Therefore it is a wise idea to make spending time in nature a daily habit, so that it becomes a part of your children's habits too. This can seem daunting at first, especially for homebodies or those who enjoy being on the go, but I can guarantee that daily time outdoors will improve your mental health and allow you to develop a nice and healthy foundation for creating an active outlet to run to in times of stress or grief.

When I was a young mother of two busy little boys, I made a commitment to get them outdoors every single day, rain or shine. At the time we lived in a city, so the woods were not at our fingertips; however, we still spent a good chunk of each morning walking to and from the park, climbing trees, identifying birds and plants, and just enjoying the fresh air. After a few months of this habit, I found myself longing for more. I discovered there was a small trail near a creek that was not covered in concrete and landscaping. We started walking that little hike on the weekends so Jason could join us. He noticed how much it helped him mentally, and the time spent together was precious. I am still convinced that this practice begun during the short time we lived there helped develop an intense connection to nature that quickly became a foundation for Jason and the boys.

Now Jason schedules a day every month or two to retreat up into the mountains alone. He takes his Bible, journal, and lunch and unplugs for the entire day, soaking in the peace and beauty of nature. He typically schedules this time to maintain his mental health and upkeep before he's emotionally pushed to go there. This is a habit that is not always convenient, mind you, because if he's up in the mountains alone that means I am with the children alone! However, it is necessary to keep him refreshed and present with our family. I know a large percentage of men struggle with video game addiction or pornography, and my heart breaks for their inner need that isn't met. They are searching for both visual and physical fulfillment and emotional detachment from the realities of life and were never given the proper tools to know how to manage such needs.

When we are in nature with our children, I make sure to call attention to what it does to their hearts and souls, so that when they are adults, they will be able to pull from these experiences a piece of truth. I may say, "Everyone take a big, deep breath of fresh pine air. We are here to get away from our daily chores and activities. This is our time to enjoy this beautiful gift of creation and not think about anything else!" I have had my children journal about what they observed in nature, what it has done for them, and how they felt when they returned home. We discuss how important it is to disconnect from the busyness of life and connect with nature. And sometimes I tell them to remember the feeling of freedom and peace and to write it on their hearts so that, when they are on their own and dealing with adult issues, they will remember there is a place of refuge.

Nature as a Teacher

The more time you spend in nature, the more you can learn from it. I believe the connection we have established by being consistently outdoors has given us a broader and more whole educational, mental, emotional, and spiritual experience in our home. Nature has the ability to shape your character just by taking part in it.

Humility and Service

One day, on one of our hikes, we identified all the purposes of a tree we could think of. A tree provides homes for animals, food for both humans and animals, shade for the weary, lumber, paper, fresh air, and so on. The list kept growing, as did our awareness of all that one humble tree had to offer us. We discussed the life cycle of a forest and how fires are often necessary so that new growth can take place and the ecosystem can thrive. While we considered what a tree had to offer us, we also examined the idea of sacrifice. Certain trees become cradles for infants, others become wagons, some are turned into rakes and shovels, and many are used for large, important buildings. What a great lesson in humility and sacrifice!

Our hikes are much different now that the children are older. They pay attention to the forest and its layers as well as come up with creative stories for the fate of specific trees. We talk about being used of God and what our purpose may look like—but whatever it is, we are to be willing and humble in heart. To serve others and use our gifts and natural abilities to care for those around us. Just as a tree can provide shelter in a storm, we should be able to help comfort those in need. I'm not sure we will ever look at a tree again without feeling the spiritual impact of service, humility, and sacrifice.

Peace and Patience

Everett, my second child, has a strong and passionate connection with nature. I have watched him sit very still on the peak of a cliff and just observe, taking it all in for long periods of time. Often I will ask him his thoughts after such a time, and he will tell me that's when he feels the most calm and close to God. What a gift to find that peace so early in his life. I am confident that by continuing to let the outdoors be his place of serenity, he will be able to use nature as an escape when his life gets more complicated as a young adult, rather than turning to unhealthy forms of escape.

Learning about nature is an ongoing task, and observing can require a lot of patience. I remember a situation at the tide pools a few years ago. We arrived at what should have been a prime time to discover life, yet we were having a hard time finding anything. Everett was the one to suggest that we sit and wait. He mentioned that perhaps our feet were vibrating the sea creatures' homes, causing them to find cover. Sure enough, after a few minutes of quiet and stillness, crabs began to come out, anemones opened, and the pool took on various vivid colors. It looked completely different than it had only three minutes prior!

Building or making anything without tools also requires a lot of patience. We have spent time building forts, sandcastles, shelters, and weapons with the challenge of not using anything man-made. We have discussed how God created a purpose for everything, yet society has tried to improve it. This has brought up a lot of healthy discussion as to which strategy we prefer. We all agreed that we can get a lot more done when using tools, but the result is less fulfilling. Adopting a patient attitude requires a lot of hard work and focus. Leaving children outside for long periods of time allows them to build up their tolerance for the creative process, which requires slow and methodical decision-making and results in a higher level of peace. In our household, if the children are restless or struggling with doing their work, we tend to look up some form of primitive skill as inspiration, and I release them outdoors. Hours later they will return refreshed and ready to focus. Nature sure does bring out the peace and patience in us, which can then encourage us to be more effective in our daily tasks.

Work Ethic and Prudence

Have you ever had the opportunity to observe a bird making a nest? Or beavers building a dam? What an admirable work ethic animals naturally have! God has created them to be able to take care of themselves, with innate abilities to find food and shelter, to reproduce, and to handle many of nature's elements. Beyond the absolute awe of nature's aesthetic is the miracle of wildlife's ability to survive. The children and I have a lot of fascinating discussions about how we are technically mammals just like some of their favorite wildlife, and we should be able to survive without outside influence. Of course, it's a long shot this day and age, but I do believe there is a reason we are so drawn to tales of the primitive days of the pioneers: we are inspired by their motivation to survive, their incredible work ethic, and their commendable prudence.

I can certainly say that through a lot of the literature we have read, the children have become more motivated and harder workers. They have been able to remove themselves from their own very comfortable world and imagine themselves in a different time or setting, or sometimes even as a different mammal. By doing so, they tend to gain a better understanding of the true value of work as well as utilizing everything nature has to offer through their best efforts. A small example is when my two older boys once realized that the birdseed we left in a moist and open container had turned to fodder. You can imagine the excitement when they found the chickens fighting over it, realizing it now had doubled in its purpose as feed for the chickens. They started setting aside extra birdseed, created their own little sprouting farm, and figured out a prudent way to feed our small brood. Years back, my good friend read *Farmer Boy* by Laura Ingalls Wilder with her son, and they were so inspired by the family's work ethic that they decided to get up at five o'clock every morning for two weeks to dig a drainage ditch together. In exchange for a lot of hard work, her son and his father were rewarded with large, delectable breakfasts similar to those described in the book. It has left a lasting effect on him, so much so that he begs for those early mornings of work again.

Giving my children enough time in nature has allowed them to connect with how God created and equipped us to survive and thrive. We may never have the opportunity to be self-sustaining or live off woodland seeds and wildflowers, but we certainly can learn about survival and encourage our children to observe wildlife habits while gleaning from their natural and God-given work ethic and prudence.

Awakening and nurturing a child's innate desire to take part in nature and learning from nature itself has been a large part of our family culture and how we personally connect as a family. There are many lessons to be learned by observing, and what a delight to be able to apply them to our lives!

FOR FURTHER READING

Humility and Service

The Giving Tree by Shel Silverstein

The Trees of the Dancing Goats by Patricia Polacco

A Single Shard by Linda Sue Park

Peace and Patience

My Side of the Mountain by Jean Craighead George

The Yearling by Marjorie Kinnan Rawlings

Owl Moon by Jane Yolen

Work Ethic and Prudence

The Little House series by Laura Ingalls Wilder

Little Britches and Man of the Family by Ralph Moody

Parables of Nature by Margaret Gatty

Nature as an Activity

When we had our first child, Carter, I remember watching the dynamics of Jason's uncle's family at holiday get-togethers. They were much further down the parenting journey than we were, and both Jason and I recognized something within their family that we wanted in ours. All of their children loved music, sports, and the outdoors, and most importantly, they loved being together. It was incredibly inspiring to be in the presence of parents who enjoyed being with their teens and teens who enjoyed being with their parents. We often bombarded them with questions so that we could learn from their parenting. I will never forget asking them about family hikes. It seemed that their teens loved hiking together, and I asked how they had cultivated it. They responded that, for many years, the children never wanted to hike. In fact, they would have rather played with the neighborhood friends, but family hiking was a habit the parents made sure to establish.

Years later, when they were in their teens and their social lives took over, the kids actually asked to go on family hikes, as it was a habit that had created a safe place to talk and connect as a family. They are all adults now and are very active. When they come together for holidays, you can usually find them hiking.

Jason and I knew we wanted this to be a part of our family culture too. We saw the benefits it brought to their family and wanted to begin the same habit with our own. We started with short, manageable hikes on Sunday afternoons, and have since moved up to weekly hikes totaling up to eighteen miles.

One of the benefits of hiking is that it is free. When you have a large family, many activities, such as going to the movies or catching a game of mini golf, can quickly drain your bank account. Hiking is something we can all participate in at little or no cost. It is also a lifelong activity. Many times we will see people well into their eighties out on the trails, enjoying the scenery and getting some vitamin D. This specific habit has very few physical restrictions, as you can adapt a hike based on terrain and elevation. When we consider our children's activities and how they will serve them in the future, hiking is one that we know they can take with them into old age, which gives greater purpose into forming the habit now.

I know that hiking can seem overwhelming with little ones. When we started this activity with our children, it was not as romantic as I had imagined. There was whining, crying, scratched knees, tired legs . . . and that was just within the first five minutes! Jason and I learned that in order to make this a lifelong habit with our family, we needed success from the start. We began with very short hikes, often bringing an Ergo carrier and/or a jogging stroller if the trail permitted. We knew our children's limits, and we would progressively add a little distance or more challenging terrain each hike so they could slowly adapt and grow. We would celebrate each new feat as a family, and it seemed for years that we were stuck under two miles. But something happened. Our children grew, and pushing their limits went from adding an extra five minutes to adding an extra five miles! Of course this didn't happen overnight, but these practices build on each other, and you will find that your children's endurance can quickly outgrow your own.

Our hiking adventures have been shared through Instagram for years, and the main response I get from moms is concern about wildlife. They often ask how we handle being so far from civilization. Educating ourselves has been an effective tool in managing the unknowns. We have spent many hours poring over survival books and maps and informing ourselves about different wildlife. For example, rattlesnakes, mountain lions, and bears are typically considered the greatest threats to hikers in our area. However, if you spend time reading about each animal or amphibian, talking to a ranger, or interviewing seasoned veterans of the outdoors, you will find that these creatures are no more of a threat to you than you are to them. All three want to avoid human contact as much as possible. If you respect them, they will respect you.

We learned that you are more likely to be killed by a cow, dog, or deer (through vehicular impact) than you are by a bear, mountain lion, or rattlesnake. The majority of the few rattlesnake bites that happen each year occur when someone is handling the snake. The remaining bites happen when someone is walking over a log and surprises the snake. Taking that knowledge, we apply it to our hikes. Typically, whoever is leading the pack carries a walking stick and knows how to jump over rocks or logs in the trail accordingly to warn any potential snake. But that's being extra cautious. Snakes will typically feel the vibration of an upcoming group and flee before anyone even sees them. If a snake bite does occur, all of the children are aware of the steps that must be taken in order to survive.

Let me remind you that the chances of wildlife affecting your beautiful hike are very slim, so it's best to read the facts to keep your fear to a minimum. We want to raise children who are confident in nature. Educating them is one of the better ways to enable their confidence. Observation is another. As previously mentioned, teaching children to be still and observe provides many benefits spiritually and mentally, but it can also help them survive.

There was a situation a few years ago when I allowed my two oldest boys to run ahead of us on our hike. At the four-mile mark, there was a Y in the trail, and they did not know which way to go. Rather than waiting for me and the younger children (which would have been the right thing to do!), they continued on the trail but chose the wrong direction. After a mile or so of knowing something was off, they sat down and observed their surroundings. They knew the lake we were hiking to was northeast of the trailhead, yet based on the time of day and the direction of the trees' shadows, they realized they were heading west. They turned around, ran back to the Y before we'd even arrived, took the correct trail, and beat us to the lake! Their powers of observation potentially saved them from a wilderness catastrophe.

I would encourage anyone who plans on making hiking a part of their family culture to read up on such issues as local wildlife, wilderness first aid, cardinal directions, and hypothermia and hyperthermia. These are all helpful, relevant subjects.

Here are our best hiking tips and tricks:

Take rewards. You'd be surprised how many extra miles you can get out of a baggie of chocolate chips!

Have a backpack for everyone. Starting with a mini backpack, which may only carry a few snacks, will get your child used to carrying extra weight. This habit is beneficial for longer hikes when more water, food, and supplies are required.

Invite friends. Not only does this enable you to spread the joy of nature and exercise with friends but you are providing extra gumption for your children to press

56

onward, as they'll be socially distracted the whole time.

Choose smart supplies. We try to keep our supplies to a minimum. Band-Aids, a pocketknife, lip balm, water, a lightweight field guide, and minimal snacks are our typical contents. A bandanna has multiple uses, so we are sure to have a few available. They are useful for bandages, covering the neck in intense sun, a bag, cold compress, cordage, and much more. Having a minimalist approach allowed us to transition from day hikes into overnight backpacking fairly easily as we had figured out which items are a necessity versus those that are convenient but not required.

Use a map. Make sure your children are familiar with map use. Use a map to plan your hike, highlighting certain noticeable elements such as creeks or peaks. Seeing the terrain from a bird's-eye view helps in the observation process as children experience walking through what they have already planned out. If we are going deep into the backcountry, we will take a map with us to help determine which direction to go. While trail apps and phones have become convenient, be aware that they are not always reliable and can often fail you. Knowing how to read a physical map is a skill that should not be overlooked and should be the preferred guide for unknown areas or backcountry backpacking.

Allow one complaint. We borrowed this idea from a friend: the children get "one complaint" the entire hike. It can be so easy to complain of being hot, tired, or out of breath the entire time. We allow one complaint, and make sure to warn them that it better be worth it! This somehow makes them question just how uncomfortable they really are. They usually make it through the whole hike without lament because they're waiting for it to get bad enough to use their allotted complaint. By the end of the hike, they question whether it was even that bad—or at least most of them do.

Take a field guide. Taking a field guide along helps children identify plants and animals. This is not just for observance and knowledge but also for awareness of what is edible and not. We constantly try to equip our children to be capable of surviving, should anything ever happen, and being able to decipher with confidence what is edible and what is not can be a lifesaving skill. As the saying goes, "By failing to prepare, you are preparing to fail."

4

SIMPLICITY

The more you have, the more you are occupied. . . . But the
less you have, the more free you are.

Mother Teresa

What an opportunity we have as parents to be able to set up
our children's home and learning environment, but more importantly, we have the privilege of creating a place of safety,
warmth, and comfort that will carry them through some of
their most memorable times. As I come from a very simple
home and background, many of my memories of home are
based around the comfort of its order and peace. I know order
and simplicity are not for everyone, but I would like to share
how our philosophy of keeping a simple environment in our
home has provided our children with the mental and physical
room to thrive in extraordinary ways.

Though we made such choices for the sake of our children, both Jason and I received an unexpected gift of added peace as we navigated through those years in the trenches. Each family has different needs, and I understand that some of these practices may seem extreme, but my hope is that by considering some of our strategies for simple living, you may be able to find the right balance of simplicity and comfort in your own home so that your family may thrive as well.

Toys

Shortly after our oldest son, Carter, turned nine months, we realized how easily he became overstimulated. As he was our firstborn, we had been showered with gifts. I had just about every baby gadget and gizmo: the bouncer, the walker, the Exer-Saucer, and all the LeapFrog light-up toys. I started noticing that the more he moved from toy to toy, the unhappier he would get. However, if I set him on the kitchen floor while I prepared dinner and gave him a few canned goods, he would play contentedly for up to an hour.

I began putting the toys away and leaving only one out for him to play with at a time. It was amazing to see how content he was with just the one toy. In fact, rather than pushing a few buttons and then moving on, he would start inspecting every part of it. Giving him less was providing him with more observation skills.

It was a quick lesson for me in the art of simplicity, and Carter responded very well to it. After we had our second son, Everett, I had to adapt to meeting the needs of two babies and figure out how to manage a busier household. Multiple toys started coming out again, the baby swing and walker reappeared, and

Carter's tiny toy basket turned into a toy section. Some days I felt really frazzled and couldn't quite figure out why.

During that season, I remember picking up a book on Waldorf education at the local library. In one of the chapters, the author spoke about Steiner's philosophy on natural materials in the home and classroom. Steiner believed that, from birth, a child should only be exposed to materials made from the earth's beauty and natural textures. While I didn't agree with the entirety of Steiner's philosophy, the idea of introducing my infant to the pureness and beauty of the natural world really resonated with me.

I decided to remove anything that was battery operated or plastic, and when birthdays or Christmas came, I asked both sets of grandparents for open-ended toys made of natural materials. Open-ended toys do not have one single purpose. A train has one purpose—to be a train—but a simple wooden block can be a train, an animal, a wall, a person, and so on. By keeping only open-ended toys such as wooden blocks and play silks around, I noticed my boys began using them for many purposes and naturally gravitated toward more imaginative play.

Once we were more intentional about our toy collection, this minimal and natural philosophy started becoming a part of our entire home environment. At that time I also began to notice some differences in Carter's neurological processing compared to other children, so I read a lot of books on autism and sensory processing disorders. I found, through alternative healing resources, that many therapists recommend natural toys and fibers in the home, as synthetic materials cannot absorb sound or energy.

Synthetic materials can cause sensory overload in a child, whether the child struggles with sensory issues or not. Natural

NATURAL TOYS

These are the toys we had in our home when the children were younger:

- unpainted wooden blocks
- unpainted wooden play kitchen with wooden plates and food
- play silks
- wooden barn

toys and fibers, such as wood and wool, can absorb sound and energy, allowing the body to process them on an as-needed basis rather than having a ricochet-type reaction. By eliminating plastic toys and materials, you are also ridding the home of extra energy and stimulation that may play a negative role in the home. Being mindful of the materials in your home can impact the living environment in positive and peaceful ways.

The wonderful part about choosing natural toys is that they are beautiful to look at and are of heirloom quality. I do not save many sentimental things, but the children's toys are now stored in closets for my future grandchildren because of their timeless purpose and quality.

By the time our third child, Scarlett, arrived, we had a pretty good gauge on what we needed to care for an infant. We did not need a walker, a bouncy chair, or a swing, but just a simple sheepskin and a linen sling. I didn't realize that this decision would not only declutter my home, encourage creativity, and help Carter's sensory needs but also improve baby Scarlett's strength and development, as she spent much more time on her tummy rather than being held upright and contained. The big boys played for hours outside with sticks and rocks, and my home felt peaceful again. And it was a good thing we had gotten into a rhythm of simple living again, because shortly after Scarlett turned one, we bought a small, 1,200-square-foot home—and then discovered I was pregnant with twins!

The following eight years in that home contain some of our most treasured memories. We had five children under the age of five in a quirky house with no garage that sat on a few acres. Because of our home's size and layout, there was little storage, and we had to be incredibly minimal and intentional with what came into our home. Making daily decisions to simplify began to mold many aspects of our home culture.

Clothing and Household Goods

I also began to realize that the children did not need multiples of every type of clothing. The more clothes they had, the more laundry we did. I started seeking out higher-quality clothing and only buying the basic minimum. For example, each child had two pairs of jeans, two pairs of shorts, one swimsuit, one pair of pajamas, and a few different shirts. If clothes needed to be washed, I would wash them in the evening so they were ready the following day. We became selective about when we washed clothing, making sure that an item was visibly dirty before throwing it in the dirty clothes. This practice taught the children to think about and assess their clothing before they just threw it in a dirty clothes bin. To this day, our wardrobes are minimal, and we wash about one to three loads of laundry per week as a family of seven. But I will be honest: teenage boys tend to have low standards for "clean."

One of the things we discovered about wearing the same types of clothing over and over is that selecting neutral, classic styles makes it less obvious that you have worn the same shirt to church three weeks in a row. Also, though I didn't realize it at the time, because a lot of our clothes were in simple, natural colors, this neurologically helped my son Carter, as there wasn't additional visual "noise" for him to process. It helped me as well. Raising five young children in a small home can be incredibly loud and stressful at times. Having the children dressed in neutral colors was another way for me to increase my mental and emotional capacity for all our daily activities, because my visual stimulus was not challenged in this way. I know it may be very radical to think that dressing your children in calm colors will make a difference in your attitude, but I encourage you to try and see what happens as a result. A fellow veteran homeschool mother, Cindy Rollins, mentioned in her book *Mere Motherhood* that dressing her children in attractive clothes made her like them more.[1] I can completely resonate with that statement! Now that the children are older and have their own opinions on what they wear, they tend to gravitate toward simple, neutral clothing as well, although one has taken the neutral part a tad too far by wearing camouflage on the daily.

As a large, young family our budget was very tight. We made most of our food from scratch, purchased a lot of it in bulk, and were basic when it came to ingredients and housewares. Once we experienced the peace that comes with simplicity, we learned to view everything through the lens of efficiency and necessity. One example: I realized we owned more dishes than we needed, and by having more than just the basics, we were wasting water, time, and space by constantly washing and using new dishes. We eliminated all of our dishes except for seven wooden bowls, and we ate every meal in those bowls! We each hand-washed and dried our own bowl and silverware after eating, and they would be ready for the next meal. Because we were so efficient with our housewares, our sink was always empty and there was less work for me to do as a mom. During that time, we never even used the dishwasher, as there weren't enough dishes to fill it. When we had friends and family over, we simply used paper plates. Having paper plates available freed up time for me to socialize with our company instead of washing the dishes.

I learned how to make simple household cleaners and necessities from ingredients such as coconut oil, lemon, and baking soda. Using those few ingredients for multiple purposes created organized cabinet spaces and made more room in the budget for healthy food. We bought soap and shampoo/conditioner when needed, so there was never a surplus that had to be stored. This simplicity journey may sound a little obsessive, but with so many loud and active young children, I found it was an absolute relief to not have added traffic in my mind and in my home. It freed up the mental and emotional capacity for me to be present with my children and to be a joyful wife.

I am not saying that one cannot be present or joyful while having an extra set of dishes or a backup shampoo bottle, but I would encourage you to make mental notes about the things you see that bother you or trigger emotions you may not want to experience, specifically in front of your spouse or children. When I meet moms who tend to feel frantic or frazzled, my first question is not about their marriage or even their children but about their home environment. Is there a great surplus of things in the home? Food, clothing, toys, housewares, and even cleaning supplies, when purchased and stored in excess, can cause an abundance of stress and anxiety because those items take up physical and mental space. Just because you may have room for excess doesn't mean that shelves and closets need to be filled.

In fact, researchers at the Princeton University Neuroscience Institute conducted a study that relates directly to mental health and uncluttered living. Their conclusion was that if your environment is cluttered, the visual chaos restricts your ability to focus and process information. If the environment is simple and organized, "research shows that you will be less irritable, more productive, distracted less often, and able to process information better with an uncluttered and organized home and office."[2]

I have a few guidelines I developed back in the days of having little ones that, surprisingly, I have kept, even though our homes since have varied in size and storage space.

- If you purchase something new and you do not wear it or use it within a week, you will likely not wear or use it often, and therefore it should be returned.
- If you have not used or worn an item for two months, and it's not a seasonal item (like a winter jacket or swimsuit), donate it. You will likely never use it or wear it again.
- If you don't like something, get rid of it.
- If it doesn't serve a purpose, get rid of it.
- If you don't currently need it, don't buy it.
- If you really want something, budget for it and wait until you have available cash to buy it.

- If you're shopping for furniture, check thrift stores first, as vintage furniture is higher in quality.
- Quality always trumps quantity.

By following these standards, I began to look at all purchases with much better intentions. This process saved me from impulse buying or from being swayed by a good sale. It also kept our cabinets from becoming stuffed with products I would forget about and closets full of clothes that would never be worn. While this lifestyle offered peace and serenity within the home, I was surprised and encouraged to find that it also grew creativity within our family.

One year, I had a grand plan for a bonfire area, and I impulsively purchased a pair of outdoor chairs because they were deeply discounted. They weren't exactly what I wanted, but the price was so tempting that I caved and brought them home. For weeks, every time I walked by them I recalled how much I disliked them. Weeks of being annoyed with something I didn't like caused unneeded traffic in my mind. One evening, the children and I were celebrating winter solstice with a fire. There were only those two chairs available but there were six of us celebrating, so Everett gathered some firewood rounds to serve as chairs. I loved the rustic and simple look of the rounds so much that we used the weekend to grind and sand seven of them to the appropriate height and texture. I ended up reselling those two chairs and was then, finally, satisfied with the visual result of our new firepit area. Not only did I get my money back but the alternative cost only time. It was another lesson in avoiding impulse buying and waiting for a creative alternative to show up.

I can share story after story of how following these guidelines changed my outlook and perspective on homemaking. What

I want to clarify, though, is that it took and continues to take learning experience after learning experience to develop this type of simple lifestyle. It doesn't just happen, nor does it continue naturally. It's a discipline. What we do may not be for everyone, but if you are lacking peace in your home, I would encourage you to take inventory of what is in your closets, cabinets, and even out on the floor and on the walls. Do they send you messages of stress and frustration? If so, it's time to purge and come up with a system that works for you and your family. This doesn't mean you need to replace things, either. Oftentimes, a purge can leave a peaceful space that never needed to be filled.

Anytime I purge our closets or garage, I am reminded of Matthew 6:19–21:

> Do not lay up for yourselves treasures on earth, where moth and rust destroy and where thieves break in and steal, but lay up for yourselves treasures in heaven. . . . For where your treasure is, there your heart will be also.

It's a quick reminder that nothing we own here on earth has eternal value, and that I should hold loosely to all that we acquire. In the end (or beginning), none of these earthly things matter.

Sports and Activities

Like many young families, Jason and I were excited to jump into soccer Saturdays with our preschool-aged children. The whole town gathered at the fields. The children wore oversized jerseys, and the parents cheered from the sidelines. It was fun—but also busy and taxing for our family. Jason coached two teams, which prevented us from having dinner together most weeknights. We spent all day Saturday at the field in the hot sun, with staggered games and tired children.

As we became more conscious of what things we brought into our home, our bodies, and our minds, we also started taking note of our schedule and our family rhythm. By choosing soccer Saturdays, we were compromising what we valued most as a family, which was hiking in the high country and spending time in the forest as a family. We decided to do a test run and not sign up for any organized sports or activities for an entire year.

That year was game-changing for us. We exposed the children to all different types of trails, rivers, swimming holes, and secret locations. We had dinner together nearly every night and had time to create new traditions like winter solstice bonfires and family work days on Saturdays. One evening, while at a friend's house for a barbeque, we were talking about sports and how we missed our soccer family but also about how we had been enjoying the year off. Our friend suggested that we try skiing, as it fulfilled the need for athletic activity but was noncommittal and something the family could do together. He sent us home with a few sets of skis and boots. The children loved it, and we soon realized that skiing gave us more quality time with our family than sitting on a sideline did. Throughout that year, I scavenged thrift stores and eBay to outfit our entire family for the slopes and even managed to secure a trade with our local ski resort when I offered my photography skills in exchange for season passes. Skiing has become the favored activity for our whole family and is a sport I hope to participate in with my future grandchildren.

One experimental year of taking a break from organized sports turned into three years as we became extremely protective of our family time. We tried out other activities that could be done as a family, such as lap swimming, tennis, watersports, rollerblading, and golf. Not every activity turned into a lifelong sport, but I am grateful for all the time we spent together while trying new things. I will always hold those three years close to my heart, as they were filled with so many special memories and intentional time.

As appealing as it may be to cancel everything and hunker down with your family, there are some developmental and individual needs that must be considered. After our three-year break, our oldest boys were entering preadolescence. After prayer and observation, we realized they both needed a physical outlet, somewhere for all of that growing testosterone. We decided to join soccer again, as it was familiar and they had an athletic history to pull from. They both fell back in love with the sport and have continued playing since. I share this because when something works for a time, and you become passionate about it, it's easy to have a "purist" mentality. But sometimes your convictions can cloud your view of the needs of your family, which is what we struggled with when we decided to join organized sports again.

Now that we are back in that sports world, our eyes have been opened to the reality of how easy it is to overschedule our children. According to one study conducted in England, 88 percent of primary school–aged children participate in extracurricular activities four to five nights per week.[3] If your household has more than one child, your entire week will be spent out of the home, and your children will end up mentally exhausted.

Athletic injuries in children due to muscle overuse are up tenfold in the past decade. Sports are starting younger and getting more intense, at a level that children cannot keep up with physically.[4] Another study shows that more than 70 percent of children quit organized sports by age thirteen, mainly because they no longer enjoy it, due to the stress and level of commitment. Many sports require year-round commitment and exclusivity and are no longer about the fun and the learning experience but about earning college scholarships and being the best. These reasons may be opportune for some, but for the majority of children, college scholarships and an MVP award are not realistic. The mental weight placed on a child in such an environment will nearly always drive them to quit. The lack of balance in youth sports is disheartening and something to be aware of for the sake of our children's mental and physical health.[5]

Anytime an opportunity for an activity comes up, Jason and I have extensive conversations about how it will affect the family. We discuss scheduling, logistics, price, and the emotional needs of all of our children, not just the child the activity is for. We have been made fun of (lovingly) by some of our friends for protecting our family time and have been called "too intentional," but I will never regret the quality time we've spent together as a family, nor would I second-guess all of the effort such conversations have taken in our decision-making.

Every year is a dance of assessing the developmental and emotional needs of our children as well as the core convictions of our family. But through experimenting and observing, we have found a good stride, allowing the children to participate in one to two organized sports a year as long as there is ample time for rest and regrouping for our family in between. We also have chosen to limit the options for organized sports so that we have specific seasons in which all the children will play the same sport at once. This has helped significantly when Jason or I coach, as we can schedule the practices to be on the same evenings and provide for more open family nights in between. It also makes for fun opportunities to play a family sport together, as everyone is equipped and passionate—albeit we can get quite heated and competitive!

Homeschooling

While our intent behind homeschooling was never about simplicity, I was surprised to see how this educational choice has affected our family in the same way that switching out our toys did. When we decided to homeschool, I was reluctant for many reasons, but my biggest fear was that I would be burned out by the end of each day and that would affect my relationship with my children. At the time we started, Carter was eight and the twins were only two. I had three toddlers and two school-aged children. It seemed busy and exhausting. However, shortly after starting our new venture, we discovered it was a much more peaceful option than sending our two boys to school.

The morning rush disappeared and evening homework stress was no longer an obstacle. There were no volunteer hours to track, and I wasn't responsible for donating time or materials for school birthday parties, plays, and fundraising events. Our days fell into a simple routine that included slow mornings, rhythmic afternoons, and wide-open evenings to spend together as a family. What I thought would be chaotic and stressful ended up being the most pleasant, nourishing decision for our family.

Carter, who I was the most concerned about with homeschooling, thrived in a low-stimulation environment where he could be stretched academically while staying in the comfort of a simple and peaceful place. Everett, who wasn't as interested in academics, had ample time to explore outside and learn about the natural world. My toddlers began learning poetry and the art of sitting quietly while I read aloud classical literature. I was able to pull from some of my favorite methods of homeschooling and apply them to create a simple, all-inclusive educational philosophy in our home. I took the guideline "quality always trumps quantity" I had learned to exercise in my homemaking and applied it to my homeschooling, which became very natural as I was already used to simplifying everything for efficiency. The longer we homeschooled, the more confident I became that it was God's plan for our family, as homeschooling was never something I had aspired to do.

I understand that homeschooling is not for everybody. We assess our children's needs and our family's needs every year to see what would be best, as we never want to be closed off to other school options. But, as part of our assessment, we consider how it would affect our family time together, the impact it would make on our relationships at home, and the shift the children would experience in their education. So far, our answers have prompted us to continue to choose homeschooling. Even with its challenges, homeschooling falls in line with our standards of simplicity and efficiency within the home.

Throughout the years, I have had the privilege of meeting and knowing many families able to keep a level of simplicity in their home without homeschooling. Some are single parents, dual income parents, or have children in multiple schools due to different ages and needs. One of the things they have all had in common is the ability to critically comb through their calendar and remove anything that is unnecessary. I have seen parents advocate for less homework, refuse to participate in Sunday sports, avoid sleepovers, and even have their children miss social activities such as youth group for the sake of gathering in the home and experiencing simple evenings together. It can be done, and it should be a constant conversation within the home to preserve and protect the mental, emotional, and spiritual health of the family.

WHOLE BODIES

5

FOOD

Let food be thy medicine and medicine be thy food.

Hippocrates

There's something about tackling a heartbreaking challenge that turns a mother into an advocate, which is why I'm sharing this very personal story with you. Between ages two and four, our oldest son, Carter, began having intense, anger-raging tantrums. They were very consistent, and as he got older they happened nearly daily.

We tried every kind of discipline strategy as well as different types of positive parenting techniques. I read several books, including Dr. Dobson's *The Strong-Willed Child*, in efforts to fix what was going on in our family. I created accountability systems as well as reward charts only to see them all fail, because if one day was different from the next, his outbursts would be even worse. I vividly remember one evening, after two hours of Carter kicking and screaming, I fell to my knees, weeping, completely lost as a mother. *Lord, what am I going to do?*

I prayed for guidance. The daily fits were causing walls to build between him and me, and they were also bringing confusion and frustration to his younger siblings. I heard the Lord tell me to research allergies, specifically gluten. It was the strangest thing, yet so clear. I had never considered that his behavior could have anything to do with the food we were eating. For the most part, we ate organic and whole foods, so it was intriguing to me that God would be so specific with his guidance. Yet the idea of removing gluten from our diet seemed incredibly overwhelming, and I was terrified to dive into the research.

I spoke with Jason about it, and he was very supportive since he was emotionally exhausted and at a loss as well. Out of desperation, we removed gluten from Carter's diet. Within two days, his anger began to subside. After a week, we had only experienced one tantrum. We were shocked and relieved but also a bit skeptical. Surely it couldn't be that easy! Through the research I had begun after that evening of prayer, I learned a plethora of information regarding neurological issues in relation to food allergies such as gluten, dairy, yeast, and peanuts as well as environmental factors like chemical cleaners, synthetic materials, and fluorescent lights, to name a few. I decided to remove the main food allergens from his diet as well as all chemicals and any stimulating materials and objects I could to detox and restart his system.

Within two days of removing those remaining allergen triggers, he woke up with a giant smile on his face. I asked him how he slept, and he answered, "Great!" for the first time in two years. He started willingly showing affection, which was something that had steadily decreased over the last year. His body

OUR PANTRY STAPLES

- Unrefined avocado oil
- Unrefined coconut oil
- Raw apple cider vinegar (with the "mother")
- Coconut aminos
- Unrefined sea salt (such as Real Salt)
- Almond flour
- Coconut flour
- Brown rice flour
- Gluten-free (GF) raw oats
- Guar gum
- Baking soda
- Raw shredded coconut
- Raw honey
- Pure maple syrup
- Raw cacao powder
- Coconut sugar
- Quinoa
- Wild rice
- Dry black beans
- Dry pinto beans
- Dry garbanzo beans
- Dry kidney beans
- Chia seeds
- Flaxseeds

started relaxing, and he started moving with smoother movements and greater ease. So many more things in him changed, from his level of optimism to his sleeping habits. Even his hearing became better. It was quite an impactful experience and such a relief to have our boy back.

We decided to be gluten-free as a family, and Carter was taught to avoid all pasteurized dairy, yeast, and peanuts. Such a freedom and peace entered our home as soon as we put this diet into place. I am confident that those few diet changes are what helped him function and feel better. We did not change his neurological makeup but rather were able to remove the triggers for a lot of the physical and behavioral reactions we were experiencing.

I know that this story will not resonate with every parent reading this, but I hope it brings encouragement or maybe even direction for any challenges you may be facing with your own children. From mild intolerances to major allergies, your child may be suffering from symptoms that can impact quality of sleep, ability to pay attention, behavior, sensory processing, a weakened immune system, and even personal attachment (which were all heartbreaking struggles in our situation). The last thing I would ever want to do is instill fear in any parent, but through our experience I want to bring awareness and hope.

While Carter's story has to do with specific allergens, I have also discovered much more about how food affects the body. One does not have to be allergic to a specific type of food for it to affect the body in a negative way. By learning how food can be used for medicine and medicine for food, you can help give your children a physical foundation that is strong and healthy and free from chronic conditions or autoimmune diseases, which sadly have become very common in children.

Whole Body, Whole Mind

Consuming healthy foods is not only physically beneficial but essential for mental health. The CDC once stated that by the year 2020, depression would be ranked as the "second leading cause of disability, after heart disease."[1] Psychiatrist Drew Ramsey, an assistant clinical professor at Columbia University, says, "Diet is potentially the most powerful intervention we have. By helping people shape their diets, we can improve their mental health and decrease their risk of psychiatric disorders."

Ramsey goes on to say that "The risk of depression increases about 80% when you compare teens with the lowest-quality diet, or what we call the Western diet, to those who eat a higher-quality, whole-foods diet. The risk of attention-deficit disorder (ADD) doubles."[2]

There are many other studies that link diet to mental health, but we don't need to look much further than our own families. What happens when your child comes home from a birthday party where there were ample amounts of sugar? You witness an entirely different child, one who is on a sugar high and then possibly a sugar low. The child's demeanor can change in an instant, and it's pretty obvious it was the party food and drink that caused it. Poor nutrition may not look like birthday party treats on the daily, but for an average American family, it can look like foods that do more harm than good for the body. It is important to start learning about ingredients, food processing, and the body's functions to truly understand what will benefit your child's physical and mental health rather than hurt it.

We certainly learned the hard way by walking through the process with Carter, but I am so grateful we were able to turn things around and start healing his body. Committing to a pure diet for several years not only helped restore his nervous system and his mind but his gut as well.

The Gut

The gut is now recognized in science as "the second brain." Neurologist David Perlmutter suggests in his book *Brain Maker* that "so many issues related to the gut are profoundly influential in the brain, and that a medical revolution is underway to change the way we treat brain-related disorders" such as

Alzheimer's, autism, Parkinson's, and multiple sclerosis. He says, "The really exciting news for me as a brain specialist is the fact that we are now uncovering powerful information in the gut that strongly relates to the health and viability of the brain."[3]

Understanding how important the gut is to overall mental and physical health is imperative to avoiding large health problems in the future. If the gut can keep a healthy amount of flora and a balanced amount of good bacteria, the rest of the body will function the way it was created to, including the brain. When a gut microbiome is healthy, it is able to absorb nutrients from good foods and eliminate toxins from bad foods.

When we were faced with the reality of removing gluten, pasteurized dairy, yeast, and peanuts from our diet, I was forced to look into alternative options that would help build Carter's microbiome back. I learned through research that foods from primitive cultures and traditional foods were what I should be looking for and making, because most of these meals had been created from whole, real foods before the advent of the modern food industry. Therefore, there was no such thing as fillers, GMOs, or preservatives.

These traditional foods also rely on fermentation, as refrigeration did not exist in those times. Eating fermented foods is one of the best ways to restore your gut flora, increase your vitamin absorption, and improve your immune system while also decreasing inflammatory molecules that can cause various autoimmune diseases or ailments.

Making such drastic changes to the diet can be incredibly overwhelming, but I encourage you to start small. Find a few recipes and kitchen staples to have on hand that everyone is happy with. As you watch your family flourish with the healthy

GET FERMENTING

Sprouting 101

When learning about the fermentation process, I also learned that our ancestors sprouted seeds, beans, grains, and nuts. Sprouting is essentially the process of germinating. I simply soak seeds, beans, nuts, or grains overnight in water with a few tablespoons of raw apple cider vinegar. After they soak for twelve to twenty-four hours, I then cook or serve them as usual. Sprouting awakens the digestive enzymes and decreases the antinutrients in these seeds, beans, nuts, or grains. Essentially, sprouting eliminates all the bad and replaces it with good—well, actually, nature is doing it!

Our Favorite Fermented Foods and Drinks

Sauerkraut

Lacto-fermented vegetables

Kombucha

Water kefir

changes, I'd also encourage you to read more about healing the gut, maintaining a healthy microbiome, and eliminating toxins.

Family Preparation

Involving children in food preparation and conversations about health will give them a sense of ownership over their food intake. It will also encourage them to try new foods or keep trying foods they don't care for. Just because a child doesn't like a food initially doesn't mean they have a long-term aversion to it.

Dr. Klazine van der Horst conducted a study regarding the intake of prepared food for children. She divided participating families into two groups, one in which children prepared a meal with a parent and the other in which children ate a meal their parent had prepared for them. The group that included children in meal preparation ate 76.1 percent more salad than the other group.[4] Children love being a part of meal preparation. For us, it's a time to recite hymns, poems, or Bible verses or to discuss the day. Busy hands tend to open hearts and minds, and keeping the children chopping and washing encourages meaningful conversations.

We teach our children to use a sharp knife around age five and give them softer items to chop such as zucchini and green onions. My boys loved earning the privilege of using a sharp object, and my daughter loved creating in the kitchen. As you prepare the ingredients with your children, not only will they want to try the raw vegetables they are chopping but they will be more excited to taste the finished product. Most of my children have come to love raw sweet potatoes, onions, squash, and more, simply because they snack on such foods as we talk our way through preparation.

Sometimes during our meal, the children say, "Thank you for the delicious dinner, Mom." However, when they help prepare, they look forward to saying, "Thank you for the delicious dinner, Mom, Carter, Everett, and myself!" The ownership is a reward for them, and it's always a delight for them to explore different flavors they helped create. Now that they are older, they can create meals on their own and have discovered the joy of testing different herbs and spices. Most of the time their experimentation ends up well—although there was once a memorable evening when we had cacao-flavored meatloaf, via Everett, which was not a favorite!

When I noticed how much my children enjoyed this process, I started buying children's cookbooks and introducing them to shows such as *MasterChef Junior*. This sparked a love and curiosity for food that translated into a desire to experiment and create in our kitchen. One perk that resulted from family food preparation and watching cooking shows was that the children started understanding food ratios, recipes, and seasonings. Through years of creating the same family staples and trying new ones, they now can make these meals from scratch without any direction. I didn't realize it at the time, but by including them in preparation I was working myself out of a job. Now my children prepare their own breakfasts and lunches and have dinner duty three nights a week.

As we prepare dinner, we talk about the foods we are using and the vitamins, minerals, and nutrients they contain. This helps the children understand the concept of a well-rounded diet. We also talk about all the colors going into the meal and how it would be quite imbalanced if the meal was all white or all yellow. This does not mean they always look forward to trying new foods or that they all immediately began consuming great quantities of Swiss chard or eggplant. Some vegetables are still a discipline in eating for different children, but we do require that they eat a small amount.

This process has not always been easy. There have been some battles at the table, such as when a child sat for up to two hours to avoid eating a few pieces of squash. Eventually, though, they either forget they didn't like a food or learn to tolerate it and appreciate it for its nutritional value. There are a few foods I let slide because I consider them "accessory foods," meaning they're never really a part of a main meal and can easily be removed. For example, after having August try avocados over and over, it was pretty evident he just couldn't get used to the texture and flavor. Because avocados are rarely a main part of a meal, and I also knew this dislike wouldn't be a huge inconvenience if we were at a friend's house for dinner, I gave him grace to skip them. Likewise, Carter has never been able to enjoy olives, pickles, or banana peppers. Even as a teen, he continues to try them and is still convinced they're too vinegary for him. Since none of those foods are main items in a meal, I have let him avoid them for the most part.

Flexibility and Moderation

One of our family's standards is that we won't have picky eaters. This doesn't happen naturally. It's a constant process of reintroducing foods and requiring the consumption of certain foods that we deem essential to their diet. Most of the motivation behind this is the idea of flexibility. We do not know at this point what God's specific plans are for our children, but we hope to equip them to be flexible in many areas of their life so they can adapt to whatever he has for them, whether that be a life in missions, living abroad, or marrying into a different culture. We try to expose them to different types of foods and experiences so they are better prepared for anything that may come their way.

We also want our children to be a blessing wherever we go. Part of being a blessing, in our opinion, is being an easy guest. If a family invites us over for dinner, we are flexible and don't usually make any dietary restrictions known. Keeping this level of adaptability allows our bodies to be exposed to different foods and not consider them completely foreign. However, when Carter was on a very strict diet, we did take separate food just for him, as we were in the process of healing his gut. But for the most part, we try to be as flexible as possible, even if the host's meal is not what we are used to. We are grateful for the opportunity to fellowship with others and for their hospitality.

We have found that if all of our guts are functioning well, we can handle toxins and foods we do not usually consume. Balancing clean eating with life outside of our home means that we don't entirely avoid unhealthy foods, we just need to take in toxins and sugars in moderation. The probiotics we introduce to our family within our home allow for the consumption of less healthy foods outside of our home. For example, if we have a fundraiser or function to attend that night that includes a hot dog meal with cupcakes, chips, and soda, we'll make sure the children have an extra helping of sauerkraut on their eggs that morning. They may also consume more fermented drinks during the day and double up on the vegetables. Building up the system so it can take a hit may be a strange way of looking at it, but it's our version of moderation.

When we travel, we make sure to always take some sort of fermented food and probiotic to aid in the digestion of foods our family may not entirely be used to. This balanced approach has taught our bodies and minds to adapt and also to enjoy different situations in the moment rather than being judgmental, fearful, or high-maintenance. When the children were younger, most of the food we consumed was prepared from scratch. Most of our grains, nuts, and legumes were sprouted, and all dairy was raw. This may sound overwhelming or expensive, but again, I encourage you to start small. Also, when we abruptly had to be on a very strict diet, buying in bulk and cooking from scratch ended up being cheaper than buying processed foods!

For a time, however, I became such a purist that I found myself struggling with social activities, my attitude, and my

OUR FAVORITE SNACKS

- Sprouted almonds
- Raw cashews
- Homemade popcorn with coconut oil and sea salt
- Raw almond butter and apple slices or celery sticks
- Raw veggies with homemade hummus
- Baked and seasoned kale chips
- Organic fruit
- Baked garbanzo beans
- Baked sweet potato fries
- Homemade yogurt from raw milk with raw honey
- Organic tortilla chips with sauerkraut
- Raw cacao balls

overall flexibility. Then I read Romans 14 and was convicted over the pretension I had developed as a result of my best efforts in keeping my family healthy and whole. I realized I had become judgmental, not toward anyone in particular but toward any lifestyle that did not align with mine. I was turning our healthy choices into an idol, and the only way to break it down was to be more moderate and relaxed, viewing lifestyle choices as personal preferences rather than law.

The change was liberating. I was able to give grandparents the full authority to treat the kids to whatever they desired, because I wanted them to have those special memories with their grandchildren. To this day, the children have fond memories of their grandma taking them to get ice cream, their grandpa buying candy at the gas station, and grabbing sushi after golf with their other grandfather. Jason and I began to reintroduce our own little "treats," and it was such a relief to be able to be more flexible with the children while also knowing they were well-nourished at home.

Our hope is that by the time our children leave our home, they will understand health and wellness enough to be able to make moderate decisions all throughout their lives, to listen to their bodies, and to engage in community-building meals and activities without being limited by restrictions or ideologies.

One way we teach our children moderation is through how we model food in our home. Any parent can agree that dealing with snacks is one of the most annoying parts of parenthood! If a child snacks too much, they won't eat their meals, where most nourishment takes place, but there are intermittent windows throughout the day when a child may need a blood sugar boost. When our children were young, we had a rhythm-based eating schedule that was built around our homeschool. We had a big, protein-filled breakfast, a midmorning snack, lunch, a midafternoon snack, and then dinner. Making meals and snacks around the clock became quite arduous. I needed a solution.

I started giving them the responsibility of monitoring their own snacks and meals. The children were all taught how to make eggs and power pancakes (see the recipe section in the back of the book) for breakfast and helped with dinner preparation. They also learned how to make their own snacks—and I gave them guidelines and portion examples for these, as they would have eaten us out of the house if they had free rein.

By laying out their portions and options, we put our children in control of their own snacks. I didn't get asked multiple times a day for a snack or when we could eat lunch. They simply knew

DAILY FOOD

This is what our children are allotted each day:

Breakfast: power pancakes, unlimited eggs, or leftovers from dinner; one piece of GF or sprouted toast with butter from grass-fed cows

Snacks: one granola bar and one serving of chips, nuts, or popcorn

Fruits: one seasonal tree fruit and one banana

Vegetables: unlimited

Lunch: GF or sprouted bread sandwich (with lunch meat or almond butter) or leftovers

Dinner: family-made, unless a certain child is assigned to a specific night

what the options were and could choose when and what to eat based on their needs. They were also responsible for cleaning up after each snack or meal. If they did not, their privilege to be self-regulated would be taken away. This system may not work for everyone, but it brought me so much sanity. It took off the responsibility of feeding my children all day and gave them the privilege to do so. Because they were given only certain snack options, their portions and nutrition were controlled, and we could budget accordingly while also having the assurance that they were eating a balanced diet.

It was fun to see how the children regulated their meals and snacks. Many times, they decided collectively to eat together at certain times or after specific school tasks. To this day, they are very regulated in their eating and usually decide to eat together. When each child turns thirteen, these guidelines are relaxed. As growing teens, they need more food and calories than their younger siblings do. My hope is that by this point they have learned what balanced eating looks like and can start exercising freedom in making their own dietary decisions. I still have the opportunity to monitor such decisions as long as the child is in my home. Sometimes my teens will ask for ideas about what to eat when they are ravenously hungry but don't want to snack all day. I love that they are able to understand that snacks are not filling. At this point, only a few of my children are in their teens, so it will be interesting to see if this system ends up being successful, but thus far it has brought more peace to me and more awareness and responsibility to our children.

It should be noted that some of my children have inherited my sweet tooth. Since we don't usually have dessert or sweets in the home, a few of them often take some of their hard-earned money to sports events and trips to town. They will buy sweets such as candy or ice cream, and I do not have a problem with this, as it's their own money and we are outside of our home. My hope is that by not entirely prohibiting such treats, they will approach sugar moderately in the future, but again, they are not grown adults yet, so it really is just a hope at this point and not a guaranteed outcome.

A Strong Foundation

Reading through our health journey, it may seem as if we have experienced a pendulum swing in our diet, but part of my food philosophy is that with a solid foundation, we can always rebuild or recover. Those born and raised prior to WWII are the last American generation that had a wonderfully strong foundation when it comes to health. Despite common engagement in harmful habits such as smoking, many have never had any major health issues. This is because many of them were raised on foods without preservatives, grew their own food, drank raw milk, and physically worked on the farm.

After the war, processed food became common, powdered milk was a household staple, and unhealthy oils started making their way into most products. There was a major swing in the food industry, and we have never recovered. Cancer, autoimmune diseases, heart disease, and obesity rates have all skyrocketed since then. However, many of this last generation are expected to outlive their children.[5] As they physically developed, they were fed whole foods and ate pastured meat. They used real butter and were actively working or playing at all times. Let us learn from this generation. If we give our children a strong foundation of whole foods, good fats, and gut-friendly ferments, they will surely be able to draw from that for the rest of their lives. They will develop a palate that craves meals filled with vegetables and healthy meats. They will remember what it was like to approach food from a moderate perspective, will crave the digestive consistency that comes with a healthy gut, and will, Lord willing, teach their children to do the same. But most importantly, they will hopefully outlive us!

Turn to the recipes section at the back of the book for a few of our favorite recipes we have used in our home to help restore and maintain all of our systems.

FOR FURTHER READING

Nourishing Traditions by Sally Fallon

The Nourishing Traditions Book of Baby and Child Care by Sally Fallon Morell and Dr. Thomas S. Cowan

Restorative Kitchen and Restorative Traditions by Dr. Ashley Turner

Deep Nutrition by Catherine Shanahan, MD

The Maker's Diet by Jordan Rubin

Unraveling the Mystery of Autism and Pervasive Developmental Disorder by Karen Seroussi

6

FITNESS

Lack of activity destroys the good condition of every human being, while movement and methodical exercise save it and preserve it.

Plato

Our bodies are temporary houses for us to live in while we are here on earth. Paul calls our bodies temples in 1 Corinthians 6:19–20, saying, "Or do you not know that your body is a temple of the Holy Spirit within you, whom you have from God? You are not your own, for you were bought with a price. So glorify God in your body." He was responding to acts of sexual immorality, but these verses can be used for any context in which we abuse our bodies by either sinning with them or treating them poorly. If we are not taking care of our temples, we are not glorifying God.

We have tried to make fitness a part of our family life from the time the children could walk, for the sake of them understanding the discipline of glorifying God with our bodies. We can equip them mentally and spiritually, but if they're not aware of or attentive to physical discipline, we have not done our job in cultivating the heart of a child who walks "in a manner worthy of the Lord" (Col. 1:10).

Have you ever experienced a moment where your inner thoughts and hopes were described by someone else's words? Perhaps it was a book, poem, sermon, or interview. When the children and I started reading *The Swiss Family Robinson*, I found myself rereading multiple paragraphs, describing to the children the importance of the text. Of course, what was so profound to me was irrelevant to them; they just wanted to know what happened next. But the way the author, Johann Wyss, poured out his dreams for his sons in the form of story and adventure was so beautiful and inspiring that I now consider *The Swiss Family Robinson* one of my favorite parenting books.

We are living in an era where the adrenaline rush that children so innately need and desire is achieved not through daring bike jumps and fort building, tree climbing, and adventure seeking, but through violent video games and the latest must-have apps. I refuse to let that replacement take place in our household. Wyss may have written his book in the early 1800s, but I stand with him on the hopes his main character had for his sons:

> I want to see my sons strong, both morally and physically . . . brave to do what is good and right, and to hate evil, and strong to work, hunt and provide for themselves and others, and to fight if necessary. . . . [They must] grow [to be] strong active men, powerful to repel and cope with danger, as well as agile

94

and swift-footed to escape from it. No man can be really courageous and self-reliant without an inward consciousness of physical power and capability.[1]

For our family, exercise and fitness go hand in hand with moral training.

Capable of Challenge

While we do practice exercise as a habit in our family, physical development is not limited to a daily run or workout. Part of my goal, by the time our children leave home, is for them to have experienced an array of physical challenges, including various group sports; hiking, running, and climbing in different terrains; hunting; snow and water sports; gymnastics; and horseback riding. My hope is that broad access to different types of experiences will provide them confidence and knowledge they can apply in any given situation. I know we live in a day and age where survival skills are no longer a necessity, but there is something within me that desires our children to accumulate experiences they could pull from if the situation requires.

Part of our homeschooling has always included a small amount of wildcraft study, in case our children are ever in a situation where they would need such knowledge. When the oldest boys were very young, we listened to a book called *Lost in Maine*, the true story of Donn Fendler, a boy who got lost for almost two weeks in the foggy mountains and survived. As the story unfolded, the boys started analyzing some of his choices, putting their survival knowledge into practice and placing themselves in Donn's shoes. The boys have continued to learn and use that knowledge throughout their years of hiking, hunting, fishing, and backpacking. In fact, the only form of arguing I will tolerate is when they are deciding whether a plant is edible or not!

Physical training started at very young ages for my children. One of the observations I made when my first two boys were toddlers was that the more physical our mornings were, the more well-behaved they were throughout the day. Since my day was admittedly selfishly planned around naps, I spent most of the morning ensuring they were physically active. We lived in a city at the time, so we didn't have easy access to the woods or nature. We'd start our morning by going on a jog (they would be in the jogger stroller), and for the last half mile they would run alongside me in their onesie pajamas. We'd then make breakfast and get dressed to start the day. Once we were all ready, we would bundle up and walk to the park, which was about another half mile away. They'd play for hours with friends, and then we'd walk back home. By this point they were usually exhausted. I have sweet memories of their rosy cheeks and their little voices complaining that they couldn't quite make it. But they always did—and they took great naps because of it. Our afternoons were also focused on expending physical energy. If we would be going to a restaurant, the library, or somewhere where they were required to sit still, we'd be sure to first get a good run in or play some baseball or basketball to shake all the wiggles out. It was amazing how a little physicality helped shape their ability to listen and obey.

As the years progressed, the boys started testing their physical limits by climbing taller trees, bouldering on rocks, and swimming in ice-cold snowmelt water. Their lack of inhibition was inspiring, and I knew, deep down, that it would be altered if I introduced the concept of fear to them. I let them try dangerous things. If something seemed unwise, we would talk through it. Usually they would convince me that they could jump the cliff or walk across the fallen tree that hung twenty feet above the rocky creek. Sometimes I would joke by responding, "Sure, go for it, but you'll have to pay the doctor's bill." They always followed through, but we have yet to experience a broken bone in our household!

I understand levels of caution vary with parents based on their own comfort level, so I would encourage you to discern the situation before allowing your children to attempt radical endeavors. For example, we recently had a situation where my oldest son went exploring in the forest behind our home. He loves bouldering and had found a new spot. We'd cautioned him to not boulder alone, but that day he did not listen to our counsel. He returned from his trip limping and shared with me that he had tried a special climb and had felt in his spirit that he wasn't supposed to go any higher, but he reached for one more hold. He instantly fell and hurt his foot. Thankfully he wasn't injured too badly, but it did require a trip to the chiropractor. When talking over the situation with him, he said he should have listened to God. Listen to that quiet quickening!

When the twins were toddlers, we started going deeper into the wilderness. We became addicted to finding new water holes to swim in, undiscovered waterfalls, and backcountry meadows to run in. Every single encounter with nature etched a deep desire in their hearts to spend more time outdoors and to discover even more territory. It birthed a love of maps and topography, hunting and fishing, bouldering and exploring. I have pictures of the older boys dangling their feet over the edge of Taft Point in Yosemite, which rises 3,500 feet above the valley floor. It was terrifying to watch, but they were confident and aware of their bodies.

One summer we discovered the concept of "nature's workout," using the natural landscape to create an obstacle course. I have videos of the children competing against each other over timed courses that included skipping on slippery rocks across a river, sprinting up a rocky crag, side jumping onto a tree branch, and then ending at a granite wall that had to be fingertip-scaled to the top. It was and is exhilarating to watch them constantly challenge themselves. Each time they achieve a new level of physicality, their confidence and agility grow, and I become more aware of just how capable children are of doing hard things.

On the bumpy forest road rides home, we discuss how physical training can translate to mental training. Every time they try something new or difficult, they then have that experience to pull from when they need it for a mentally or emotionally trying situation. We also talk about decision-making, and how the more they train physically, the more inclined their bodies are to make a better split-second decision on how to fall or where to land. Life decisions are the same. The more you train your mind and your spirit to make the right decisions, the easier it becomes to walk in righteousness. Those days are filled with life lessons that my children use consistently.

Years ago, Carter, then age twelve, wanted to run a full marathon with me. He had taken up the passion of running and wanted to challenge himself. I was not up for the challenge of a marathon, but I did agree to train for a half-marathon with him. Training with a twelve-year-old boy is less than ideal. He struggled with some of our longer runs; let's be honest, running for twelve miles in the rain is not fun for anyone, let alone a tween boy. I was secretly discouraged and nervous he would shut down when it came to race day. He remained committed, though, and one day we found ourselves standing in the early morning fog after a sleepless night, waiting for the starter's gun to fire. The environment was loud, busy, and invigorating . . . just about everything a child on the spectrum would loathe. The odds were against him, and I walked through a plan in my mind on how I would handle the situation if he shut down. But Carter had high hopes and placed himself in the first wave of runners based on speed. We couldn't run together due to our different projected finish times, and we were separated by thousands of runners. Nearly halfway through the race, however, I was able to spot him. He was leading a pack of grown men on their way back to the finish line. I couldn't believe it. Based on his location, he would finish the race at the unrealistic time he'd set as his goal. When I eventually crossed the finish line, I looked all around and soon found him with a giant smile on his face. He had done it. He finished with a pace of 6:58 per mile, two seconds under his goal pace. My boy had run 13.1 miles in an hour and a half, against all odds. Later that evening, when we were talking about our experiences, he told me how he'd wanted to quit during the last mile and a half. His legs went wobbly and his knees started hurting badly. He was tempted at every water stop to just sit and wait for me. But he started praying. He asked God to help him make it to the next corner, then the next. He imagined some of his favorite places in the mountains and did everything he could to distract himself from the pain and exhaustion he was facing. Carter's accomplishment was a result of a lifetime of pushing himself and knowing who to turn to when he was tired or afraid.

Angela Duckworth, a professor of psychology at the University of Pennsylvania, wrote a book titled *Grit: The Power of Passion and Perseverance*, in which she recognizes that, in our culture, we are obsessed with accomplishment but unfortunately often neglect to acknowledge the mundane effort that goes into it. She mentions a published study on competitive swimming called "The Mundanity of Excellence," which she paraphrases by saying, "Most dazzling human achievements are, in fact, the aggregate of countless individual elements, each of which is, in a sense, ordinary."[2] The heart of accomplishment is practicing faithfulness in the mundane. Let us teach our children that if we want a healthy mind, daily we need to focus on things that are lovely, have discipline in our choices, and use wisdom in our actions. If we want a healthy body, daily we need to be cautious of what we feed it, challenge our physical abilities, and monitor what we expose it to. If we want a healthy spirit, daily we need to be in the Word of God, spend time in prayer, walk in the Spirit, and look for opportunities to serve others. Let us teach our children to recognize that these disciplines will lead not only to a more fulfilling life on earth but will receive a welcome of "Well done, good and faithful servant" in heaven (Matt. 25:21). Let's train our children to be able to be resilient, push limits, and take risks!

A Family That Plays Together, Stays Together

Being active together as a family helps improve family bonding, physical health, mental health, and confidence in children. Exercise releases hormones in the body such as endocannabinoids and endorphins. Endocannabinoids work with the reward areas of the brain and improve overall mood and mental health.

Endorphins are your body's natural opioids, which are the feel-good hormones that block out pain. As a result, people feel happier after they exercise. We have our own little controlled study in our home, and I can attest to the science behind exercise and improved moods.

Every weekday morning, the kids and I run or work out. Even though this practice has been in place for years, not everyone wakes up happy to run; in fact, it still takes a lot of effort to just get them out of the house with their tennis shoes on. However, after a mile or two, attitudes drastically change. By the time we make it back to our house, the children are laughing together and carry happy dispositions back into our home. While we exercise for the physical benefits, the mental benefits have helped our household exponentially, and we have a deeper bond because of it.

A recent study from UK psychologist Janice Thompson shows that while the majority of parents agree that being active together would benefit their family, very few participate in exercise, sports, or physical activities together. Most reported that they are unable to due to schedule difficulties and lack of interest from their children.[3] I understand the struggle these families are facing, but there are still creative ways to keep that active bond with each other. You do not need to be a homeschooling family in order to make time for family activities.

One of the ways we have learned to carve out room for activity is by attending a child's sports practice or game together. Often Jason will coach soccer, for example, and then after the practice or game is over, we will keep the goals set up and play some family soccer. This has become such a habit for our family that other families have started to join in. It is such a wonderful time to spend with each other—laughing, running, and, if I'm lucky, scoring! We have years of memories playing on different fields, and I have learned a little bit about how to play soccer because of it. We have done the same thing with other sports such as baseball or basketball. If the field or court space is available, we will make it a family affair by playing together. We have varied levels of athleticism and ability in our family, but it can still be fun whether someone has the proper technique or not. Even playing kickball on the ball diamond after a baseball game is a great way to bond.

Since friends make everything more fun for children, we will sometimes plan a family soccer morning with other families. We started the tradition on the day after Thanksgiving, the day after Christmas, and on New Year's Day, and the tradition remains, even though we have moved across the country. We'll invite several families to meet on a public field, and depending on how many show up, we've had up to four games going at once! Planning such activities is not just about friendship and fun competition but is also a way to care for our bodies by staying active and pushing ourselves physically. Just because Jason and I are getting older and grayer doesn't mean we can't challenge our physicality. We won't let those young'uns take us down!

Trying New Things Together

One afternoon, I had a conversation with Scarlett just hours before she was to try out with her brothers for the summer swim team. She was nervous and afraid to start something new. She's an insightful girl and tends to ask me a lot of questions about my own experiences. When I was explaining to her about the importance of knowing how to swim well, she responded by asking me, "Well, do you know how to swim all of the strokes?" Touché. Sometimes I get so caught up in pushing my children out of their comfort zone that I forget how frightening it is to try new and intimidating things. Her question inspired me to sign up right alongside them, and I found an adult program willing to take on a beginning swimmer. I bonded so much with my children that summer because all of us were starting something new and challenging. We'd discuss our workouts and our fastest times, and we'd talk about techniques and flip turns. In the evenings, if there was a heat wave, Jason would join us at the pool and we'd do laps together, racing each other on different strokes. Swimming was difficult for all of us. It pushed us physically and mentally, and the children developed muscles in places I never knew existed. I still find myself wondering why swimming didn't do the same for me!

Also, adopting a "not yet" philosophy as a family can help contribute to an adventurous outlook on life and activities. Many times, we will decline an opportunity because we don't feel like we are capable or qualified. For example, if someone asks you if you have participated in CrossFit, rather than saying no, what would it look like to say not yet? You're then leaving the door open to further explore something new. Using this phrase as a family helps everyone know that nothing is impossible and that there is always room for growth.

Researcher Carol Dweck has a thought-provoking TED Talk titled "The Power of Believing That You Can Improve," in which she discusses the difference between a growth mindset and a fixed mindset in children.[4] If children can understand the process of growth and development, they are more prone to try new concepts and activities. This mindset encourages perseverance and stick-to-itiveness. They understand that if they push their minds and bodies past a comfort zone, they can then move into an accomplishment zone, which then motivates them to press on. This is what happened with Carter in his half-marathon. He could have easily quit when it got exhausting and uncomfortable, but Carter was used to pushing past the comfort zone. He recognized that he had to use his mental strength and his faith in order to move into the accomplishment zone. Those with a fixed mindset allow their limitations in one area to dictate their ability to succeed in another. Therefore, they get stuck and are hesitant to try new things or challenge themselves. I understand that the nature of some children is to be less adventurous or more cautious, but that does not mean they cannot adopt a "not yet" mentality. If parents are willing to partner with them by using discernment on when to push them out of their comfort zones, they are more likely to develop an optimistic view of life and a strong character.

Active Parents, Active Kids

Pushing children to do hard things is great, but if parents are not modeling the same behavior, there will be a disconnect. You may be able to require physical performance in your children, but it will likely not result in a lifetime habit unless you are practicing some sort of physical activity yourself. After an interview with Olympic triathlete Alistair Brownlee regarding his active childhood, researchers at Open University conducted a longitudinal study that assessed physical activity levels in one hundred children ages four to seven and their parents. They discovered:

> Children of active mothers were twice as likely to be active as children of inactive mothers. Similarly, children of active fathers

were 3.5 more times as likely to be active as those with inactive fathers. When both parents were active, the children were 5.8 times as likely to be active as children of two inactive parents.[5]

Imagine the statistics if the parents were involved with the children in such activities! Participating in physical activities with your children not only benefits their mood, their physical body, and their bond with you but also instills in them a lifelong need and desire to remain active. By building such a healthy physical foundation, you are creating a more holistic approach for your children to view their future with. I can't imagine an active, robust young man seeking out an inactive, pessimistic young woman as his wife, can you? The habits you form as a family will likely influence the standards your children set for their future spouses. If this all seems too daunting, think about the generation that will become as a result of creating a holistic family culture. How you participate with your children now will shape how they participate with your grandchildren later.

Some of my favorite stories of his childhood that Jason shares with us revolve around his mom taking him and a few friends out of school to ski on a perfect powder day. One time, they all gathered at the top of the ski lift and she raced the boys down the hill, beating every single one of them. Jason's dad plays tennis or racquetball multiple times a week and has for as long as Jason can remember. These active memories and habits form his outlook and perspective for maintaining an active lifestyle. I have fond memories of stretching on the floor with my dad prior to running and can remember my mom's waterskiing tricks. My kids have held all of my stepdad's half-marathon medals in their hands. Our parents' active lifestyles influenced the way we raise our children, and they are able to watch all of their grandchildren live healthy, active lifestyles as a result of their own priorities. Taking part in physical activity is essential for the future legacy of your children and their children, not to mention essential for your own health.

Not every community offers adult soccer leagues or adult swim programs, but trying new activities as a family can look as simple as purchasing some tennis rackets from a thrift store and taking advantage of local tennis courts, or downloading an app such as AllTrails and using it to find nearby hiking trails. Some of our friends spend their summers in campers by the lake, wakeboarding and waterskiing, and others participate in local 5Ks for good causes. There are so many options that can be done as a family. Don't let your current physical shape dominate your mindset. You can start something new, something as simple as a family walk after dinner or doing burpees on the back porch. Start somewhere and build lasting memories while releasing endorphins together.

Self-Control

My grandfather died at age ninety-seven. Up until a few months before his death, Grandpa ran a mile a day. I can still remember him running and, toward the end of his life, shuffling his way through that mile so faithfully. At his funeral, one of his friends shared a conversation he had with my grandpa about a month before he died. He asked him, "Russell, why do you love running so much, and how can I learn to love it?" My grandpa replied, "Are you kidding me? I hate running. Every morning, I tried to talk myself out of it, but every morning I chose to be a temple for the Holy Ghost."

Perhaps what I love most about watching my family exercise is the fact that doing so requires a good amount of self-control.

Self-control is a fruit of the Spirit that is essential to living a holy life. When Paul writes to the Corinthian church, he compares engaging in the Christian walk to the training of elite athletes: "Do you not know that in a race all the runners run, but only one receives the prize? So run that you may obtain it. Every athlete exercises self-control in all things. They do it to receive a perishable wreath, but we an imperishable" (1 Cor. 9:24–25). What Paul is saying is that the extreme level of self-control used in preparation for competing in the Grecian games should be the same level of self-control we are to use continuously in our Christian walk. Exercise is not necessarily a spiritual act of discipline, but it is a manifestation of self-control in our lives.

7

HEALTH AND WELLNESS

The first wealth is health.

Ralph Waldo Emerson

When I was ten years old, my father was diagnosed with brain cancer. I watched as he endured a complicated twelve-hour surgery and six weeks of intense radiation that caused nausea and excruciating migraines. Thankfully, he went into remission for nine years, and my siblings and I were able to have our father around throughout our childhoods at home, even though he experienced heartbreaking episodes of extreme pain. While I am so grateful for the extra years we had with him, I still long for more and wish he could have been comfortable during that time. I can't change the past, but my dad's experience and our loss sparked in me a passion for prevention and an awareness of alternative treatments for health conditions.

Not until I became a mother, though, did this passion come into play. It took a medical situation with my firstborn son to awaken the advocate within me. It sent me in search of answers and encouraged me to find solutions. I became a student of health and wellness, reading hundreds of scientific studies and books on the way the body was created to work and function. I studied primitive cultures and their ways of treating ailments and caring for their health through traditional practices. Through all of this research and learning, I came to the conclusion that we truly are to take dominion over all that God has created for us (Gen. 1:26), including herbs, minerals, plants, and animals, for they all have multiple purposes and applications we can use to the advantage of our family's well-being.

Before we begin, let me remind you that I am not a medical doctor. I encourage you to seek advice from your medical team. You may want to consider working with a naturopath and a chiropractor in addition to a pediatrician or other medical doctor to formulate plans that work for your family. Each child is different, and my experiences do not come from a medical background but from the perspective of a mother turned advocate.

Our family has adopted some alternative treatments, and everything in this chapter is something we personally use. The homeopathy and treatment we have used for our children may not be the right fit for yours, but I am happy to share what has worked thus far in our own family.

Being Barefoot

Our children have played barefoot outdoors from a very young age, which has aided their physical and neurological development. Different parts of the foot are used to grip the ground for strength and balance. When barefoot, there is no barrier between the earth and the foot when sending messages to the brain. The body adjusts its footing while walking or running over varied terrain; this physical process is called *proprioception*. Since feet are one of the most sensory-rich parts of the human body, walking barefoot allows the proprioceptors in the joints and muscles of the feet to experience controlled levels of sensory input from the surrounding environment as the body and brain are focusing on spatial awareness, balance, and coordination. This encourages the mind to be conscious and aware of the body, which contributes to higher safety and confidence in physicality.

From firsthand experience, any of my children can attest to this scientific data. When we are out hiking in more difficult terrain, if we are on granite or steep mountains, we will often remove our shoes and socks so that we can grip the rocks more efficiently. We can feel each toe working individually to grasp the surface and can almost hear the messages our ankles and soles of our feet are sending to our brain. It's pretty remarkable how we were created with tools to help in such circumstances. The children climb trees barefoot as well, and I am always more confident in their ability to climb when they are shoeless. We talk about this often, as I want them to make the connection of how their body was created.

One fall, my father-in-law requested that Everett come and blow the leaves off his roof and out of his gutters. He is not so keen on heights, and Everett's natural place is usually ten feet above ground. My father-in-law had a rope to put around Everett's waist in case he fell. But before Everett climbed up on the roof, he took off his shoes and socks and told his papa that the rope would be much more dangerous than if he was without barriers. Up went this ten-year-old boy, barefoot and with a blower, like he had been doing it his whole life. The training and experiences behind that moment bore fruit as he was completely comfortable and confident. I was as well, knowing his body and brain were capable of such a feat.

Oil Pulling

Oil pulling is an ancient Indian practice that involves swishing unrefined and cold-pressed coconut, sesame, or sunflower oil in the mouth for ten to twenty minutes daily, ideally first thing in the morning, then spitting it out. The purpose of oil pulling is to improve oral health as well as "pull out" potential toxins and bacteria that can lead to illness. When oil is swished within the mouth, it emulsifies plaque and lifts it from the teeth and gums. Coconut oil attacks the streptococcus mutans bacteria as well as oral candida because it contains caprylic, lauric, and capric acids, which are all antifungal.[1]

Oil pulling is a morning habit in our household. I can personally attest to the fact that it acts not only as a detoxifier but as a teeth whitener as well. When we are consistently oil pulling, our teeth are white, clean, and sparkly, and we also tend to stay very healthy. There was a three-year stint in which we didn't have dental insurance and were unable to pay for dental visits. I hoped and prayed that oil pulling and a healthy diet would be enough to avoid oral health issues during that time. Once we were able to afford dental visits and cleanings, I was pleasantly surprised to find that not one child had a cavity . . . a true testament to oil pulling! This is just one more habit to instill in the family that benefits not only your oral health but your physical health as well. Again, you must spit out the oil; do not swallow it or you will also swallow the toxins you are pulling. You also must spit out the oil in a trashcan or canister as it will easily clog up the pipes with extended use.

Sleep

Sleep is, by far, the most overlooked aspect of health and wellness, yet it is probably the most important, as it's an essential part of child development. A recent study done through the National Survey of Children's Health states that over one-third of American children are not getting adequate sleep, and over 87 percent of teenagers are suffering from sleep deprivation.[2] Without consistent and adequate sleep, children can suffer in significant ways.

While sleep mostly affects the body, it certainly affects the mind as well. Lack of sleep raises levels of cortisol, a stress hormone. Higher levels of cortisol in a child lead to anxiety and depression. The earlier you instill good sleep habits, the better, as the body tends to adjust to getting less sleep and therefore operates with higher cortisol levels—which means, unfortunately, that you may not see the results of poor sleep until years later.[3]

Sleep loss is linked to diabetes and obesity in children, as it affects the body's ability to metabolize sugar and trigger insulin resistance. Sleep loss may also impede physical development and decrease immunity, as the highest levels of human growth hormone and an immune-boosting substance called interleukin-1 are both released during deep sleep.[4]

Before my firstborn, Carter, arrived, I was given the book *The Babywhisperer Solves All Your Problems* by Tracy Hogg, which sat on a shelf until he was a few months old. It was at that point that we were both sleep deprived, and I also had to face the stark reality of going back to work. I needed help on how to help manage his sleep needs for myself and for his caretakers, and the book supplied it. Hogg provided extensive research on sleep that allowed me to view parenting from a different angle.

SUGGESTED SLEEP TIMES FOR OPTIMAL DEVELOPMENT (IN 24 HOURS)

Age	Hours of Sleep
0–1 year	13–15 hours
1–3 years	12–13 hours
3–5 years	11–12 hours
5–10 years	10–11 hours
10–13 years	8–10 hours

Rather than parenting out of survival and exhaustion, I wanted to parent out of confidence and understanding. By becoming aware of Carter's physical needs, I was able to start implementing a plan that assisted in his overall well-being, which ended up being exactly what he needed. After I implemented some of Hogg's techniques, a very happy, well-adjusted, and contented baby emerged.

What I appreciated most about Hogg's book was her philosophy for child-rearing, which is, "Start as you mean to go on." I quickly adopted that phrase and used it repeatedly in the early years, especially for sleep and discipline issues. It even flowed into our homeschooling journey, as habits and discipline play a large role in making the day flow smoothly and keeping characters and hearts in check.

I understand there is a lot of conflict in different parenting methods regarding sleep training and discipline. I want to make it clear that the sleep training plan we used for our children is not right for everyone. In fact, at the time, a close friend and I had a good laugh over Hogg's book: while it brought me peace and understanding, it brought her only stress and insecurity.

We are vastly different from each other, and so are our children. Some children require more sleep than others, and some may need different methods (especially when a child has experienced trauma or has a need for new attachment, such as through fostering or adoption). We must understand ourselves and how we operate in order to best meet the needs of our children. Sleep is the priority; the method should be chosen based on parents' understanding of themselves and their children.

Our methods varied from child to child. For example, my firstborn was and still is sensitive to sensory input. We often needed to take him into a quiet room before his nap and just let him be, without any stimulation. We wouldn't rock or talk to him, we would just stand and hold him still for a few minutes so he could decompress before laying him in his crib, where he would usually fall asleep immediately. If we didn't pay attention to his cues, he would quickly become overstimulated, which resulted in skipped naps, an overtired baby, and lots of crying. He relied on us to provide him with a quiet place to retreat and sleep.

My second son was very different. He could handle noise and action right up until it was nap time, but when it was time, he didn't want to be held. He wanted to be placed in his crib, where he would play, talk, or even cry for a little bit before he went to sleep. It was his way of preparing his body and mind to rest and recover.

By the time our third, fourth, and fifth children arrived, bless their hearts, we were far more active and at home a little less. Many of their naps were shorter and took place in a sling or carrier. But I always tried to give them one good, large nap at home. By prioritizing sleep and being a well-versed student of their patterns and cues, I made sure they were getting an adequate amount of rest. On days when they'd napped only in an Ergo, I prioritized putting them in bed by 6:00 or 6:30 p.m. so they could recover from the busy day in their evening sleep.

What does adequate sleep look like? Sleep studies show that every hour between sunset and midnight provides the body with deep, non-rapid eye movement (non-REM) sleep.[5] This is the most crucial time for the body to regenerate and repair itself. After nearly three cycles of non-REM, the body will then experience REM sleep, where the brain is more active. REM sleep will then cycle every ninety minutes after non-REM sleep, assuring that the body and brain are working toward development. Knowing this information encouraged me to instill earlier bedtimes for our children. As they grow up, we are more sensitive to social opportunities, but when they were younger, it was always a priority to have them in bed by 7:00 or 7:30 p.m.

Our Use of Natural Remedies

Viruses, illnesses, and infections are inevitable in an active family, but there are countless ways to boost immunity, shorten the duration, and tame the symptoms without harming the body. Most of our remedies are made by using cost-effective household items.

When Carter was a chubby one-year-old, he came down with his first cold. Then he got a fever and started pulling on his ear. I quickly set an appointment up with his pediatrician. He saw Carter briefly, looked in his ears, declared the source of pain was an ear infection, and sent us home with amoxicillin. I could not imagine putting this pink, bubble gum–flavored medicine in his pure little body. The internet was not a go-to resource at the time, so I called my midwife to ask her thoughts. She suggested trying garlic oil first to see if it would suppress the pain, and if he didn't have any symptoms after a day or two, we could avoid using the antibiotics. I pressed garlic cloves and their juice into heated olive oil, strained it, let it cool down, and placed a drop in my son's ear. Sure enough, within minutes he was relieved of his pain. After two or three more drops throughout the day, his fever broke, he slept all night, and he woke up as good as new. I couldn't believe that something in my pantry had the ability to heal my child. This experience sparked the beginning of a passionate journey of learning and understanding health and wellness.

In our quest for giving our children the most holistic treatment we could, we have tried a plethora of different natural home remedies. Nature has given us so many resources to pull from that we can't possibly use them all. I'd like to share the remedies that have worked for our family in the past fifteen years. Most of them we have used due to their cost efficiency. When there is more than one remedy listed, we either rotate treatment or use whatever option is available in our pantry.

Ear Infections

Garlic is anti-inflammatory, antiviral, and antibacterial, and it aids in the prevention of diseases and cancer. It helps detoxify the body, is a good source of vitamin C, and helps with iron absorption. It loses a lot of its nutrients when heated, so try to add to most recipes at the very end of your cooking.[6] For *garlic oil*: put two teaspoons extra virgin olive oil in a small bowl. Crush three cloves of garlic into the oil and let steep for thirty minutes. Strain and use the oil in both ears.[7] Discard any leftover oil after twenty-four hours.

Colloidal silver is a natural microbial antibiotic derived from minute silver particles suspended in water. Place two to three drops of colloidal silver in each ear. We also use colloidal silver for pink eye (two drops per eye every three hours) and for immune boosting (two to three drops orally every few hours when fighting off a virus).[8]

Melaleuca. Also known as tea tree oil, melaleuca oil contains antibacterial, antiviral, antifungal, and anti-inflammatory properties. Melaleuca is our go-to oil for anything infection related. Mix two drops with a carrier oil such as coconut or olive oil and rub on the skull bone behind the ear. Do not put in the ear.[9]

Sinus Infections, Candida, UTI, and Strep Throat

Grapefruit seed extract (GSE) can be found in health stores and comes in liquid or pill form. Grapefruit seed extract has been used successfully for many years, and its antifungal properties have been used in the agricultural industry to prevent mold. It's even used in hospitals as an antiseptic.[10] It's loaded with vitamins and minerals as well, and can even kill and prevent the growth of parasites.[11] *GSE shot*: purchase or make fresh-squeezed orange juice and add ten to fifteen drops of GSE. Mix and drink. Repeat throughout the day. Add a shot of ginger for more immunity boosting. GSE shots are appropriate for sinus infections, UTIs, strep throat, and for killing off candida.

Eucalyptus oil relieves congestion and stuffiness while reducing mucus.[12] Eucalyptus oil contains a compound called cinole, which has been found to improve headaches, nasal obstructions, and runny noses. Mix two drops with a carrier oil and put on chest, or run a steam bath and add two drops.

Sore Throat, Cold, Flu, and Runny Nose

Apple cider vinegar (ACV) is by far the most versatile, help-ful, and effective item in our pantry. ACV protects from harmful bacteria, detoxifies the liver, builds a healthy lymphatic sys-tem, flushes free radicals, increases good cholesterol, regulates blood sugar, and keeps the body's pH in place.[13] While it can and should be used as a daily supplement, we use it mostly to combat colds as soon as that "tickle" appears. *Fizzy drink*: mix two teaspoons raw ACV (with the "mother") with one packet of either Zarbee's Naturals Immune Support and Vitamin C or Emergen-C, which is a more budget-friendly option but has less-ideal ingredients. Add a cup of water and enjoy! Drink one to three times a day until the cold subsides.

Propolis is a substance bees make and use to seal cells in their hives. It's antiviral and antibacterial. If you know a beekeeper, try to purchase a jar, as propolis aids in soothing sore throats, healing cold sores, and shortening the length of a common cold.[14]

Eucalyptus oil: mix two drops with a carrier and rub on chest and bottoms of feet for headaches and sinus-related congestion.

Elderberries are known for their antioxidant properties as well as their amino acids, vitamins A, B, and C, and bioflavo-noids (which destroy the ability of viruses to infect a cell).[15] Studies have shown that elderberry juice or syrup shortens the duration of a cold or flu when taken at the onset of symptoms. Taking elderberry juice or syrup as a preventive measure can make you less likely to come down with a cold or flu.[16] For a time we were blessed to live on a property that had a large elderberry tree, which provided more than enough harvest for our cold and flu season. However, we now have to order dried elderberries online.

ELDERBERRY SYRUP

1⅓ cups	fresh or frozen elderberries (or ⅔ cup dried elderberries)
3¼ cups	water
2 tbsp	grated ginger
2 tsp	ground cinnamon
½ tsp	ground cloves
1 cup	raw honey

Combine all ingredients except for raw honey (heat will disturb its healing properties) into a saucepan, bring to a boil, then simmer until the liquid is reduced by nearly half. Remove from heat and cool until you can safely mash the berries. Strain and pour into a glass jar. Wait until the juice is only warm and then add the honey. Stir well and refrigerate for up to 6 months. Take 1 tsp a day as a preventive measure during cold and flu season, or 1–2 tsp 3 times a day when fighting something off.

Liquid echinacea and goldenseal is a dynamic herbal duo known to relieve respiratory inflammation, promote stronger immunity, and minimize mucus secretion.[17] When anyone in our home feels the slightest bit of a cold coming on, I add two or three droppers of echinacea goldenseal into the elderberry syrup and administer two to three times per day.

Epsom salt, sea salt, and baking soda bath. Epsom salt is a pure mineral compound of magnesium and sulfate linked to detoxifying and anti-inflammatory properties. Sea salt contains twenty-one minerals, including magnesium, calcium, sulfur, zinc, and potassium.[18] Baking soda is a natural alkalizer

DETOX BATH BLEND

2 cups   Epsom salt
½ cup   sea salt
½ cup   baking soda

Mix all ingredients and store in a glass jar. Scoop out approximately ½ cup and place into a hot, steamy bath. You can also add up to 5 drops of a preferred essential oil based on what your body needs relief from, be it cold and flu, skin infection, muscle soreness, or other ailments. Be sure to research different essential oils and their uses prior to testing them out in your bath!

that helps balance and detoxify the body.[19] Soaking in all three ingredients helps to detoxify, reduce pain and stiffness, encourage a good night's sleep, improve circulation, and alkalize the body.

First Aid

Calendula spray. The calendula plant is known for its healing properties.[20] We have used store-bought calendula spray to help soothe pain, itching, chapping, burns, cuts, and scrapes. In fact, I had a C-section where the doctor forgot to stitch me. It was too late to staple or stitch me once the nurses noticed the mistake. Spraying calendula on the deep, open wound allowed it to heal very quickly without infection. We use calendula spray in place of antibiotic ointments.

Chamomile and honey. We used cloth diapers for most of our children, and because of the wetness against their skin,

BOTH WORLDS WORK TOGETHER

I realize natural remedies can be looked down upon and can also be controversial. I understand the perspective on both sides, but after learning about immunology and gut health, I always prefer to treat with natural remedies first. Using natural remedies has saved our family thousands of dollars. Not one child has ever had to use antibiotics, and they have never had to suffer long visits to a pediatrician's office while not feeling well. Being familiar with a few go-to natural remedies and acting immediately can reduce your doctor visits, prescriptions, and illness in your family. However, there are times when medical intervention is needed, and I am so grateful for Western medicine when those times come. Especially when those times involve stitches, which is about every few months with four boys in the house!

Many times, natural remedies can be used in conjunction with Western medicine, just as I used calendula on my C-section opening. However, studies are showing that some medical treatments can do more harm than good, such as the overuse of prescriptions.[21] While antibiotics and other prescriptions have saved millions of lives throughout the years and continue to save lives, they come with their own risks and should be used with wisdom and guidance from a trusted health professional.

diaper rashes were common. Every week I would make a batch of chamomile tea and add raw honey to it once it cooled. I would funnel the mixture into a spray bottle and use it with either cloth wipes or paper towels to replace store-bought wipes. I would also spray the mixture onto chapped skin.[22] It immediately soothed and healed the rash. This spray can be used on poison oak and poison ivy or other rashes as well.

CHAMOMILE TEA SKIN SPRAY

5 cups water
3 tea bags organic chamomile tea
2 Tbs raw honey

Boil water, add tea, and steep for 10 minutes. Remove tea bags, let tea cool to lukewarm, and then add raw honey. Pour solution into a spray bottle.

Melaleuca (tea tree) oil. Tiny infections such as splinters and hangnails are common, but they are never comfortable. We use a drop of melaleuca oil, along with a carrier oil, on the site of irritation. It usually helps relieve pain instantly, and the infection is typically gone overnight.

Lavender oil is our go-to for soothing any burns or relieving the itch from bites or stings.[23] Add one to two drops to a carrier oil and rub gently on the site.

Arnica is a flower used in medicine as a painkiller and as a postoperative treatment to prevent inflammation, and we use it at home for bruising, muscle aches, or swelling.[24] We typically purchase arnica gel and rub it on the affected area.

Antibiotics and Gut Health

Over 60 percent of your immune system is located in your gut,[25] and over 90 percent of your neurotransmitters are produced in your gut.[26] Neurotransmitters are chemical messengers that help regulate moods, emotions, and memory. Some of the main neurotransmitters and their functions are dopamine (behavior), serotonin (mood), norepinephrine (stress hormone), and glutamate (learning and memory). As mentioned before, the gut can often be referred to as the second brain, as it houses so many neurotransmitters that play a role in your mental state. The gut is one of the most complex ecosystems, housing trillions of live bacteria. Any disturbance can cause significant effects on your health.

Antibiotics were created to block bad bacteria or to stop the multiplying of bacteria that causes infection; however, they are not capable of eliminating only the bad bacteria. They destroy both bad and good bacteria, which leaves the immune system vulnerable and imbalanced.[27] Without healthy bacteria, also known as flora, the gut is susceptible to overgrowth from other organisms, candida being the most common. Yeast candida can lead to an array of physical problems and can eventually lead to leaky gut and autoimmune disease. One contributor to yeast candida is the use of antibiotics.[28]

Antibiotics are widely overused. A recent study by the CDC confirms that at least 30 percent of prescribed antibiotics are unnecessary. Researchers found that most of the unnecessary antibiotics were prescribed for respiratory conditions caused by viruses, which do not respond to antibiotics. When antibiotics are overused, the body becomes resistant to them, and when or if they are ever truly needed, the body may not respond. According to former CDC director Tom Frieden, "Antibiotics are lifesaving drugs, and if we continue down the road of inappropriate use we'll lose the most powerful tool we have to fight life-threatening infections."[29]

For any infections or illnesses where antibiotics may typically be prescribed, we will use our natural remedies to prevent long-term side effects to the gut. If there is no way to avoid antibiotics (for example, my C-section), I try to stay calm and not worry about it too much; stress will only raise the cortisol levels, extending healing time. After I complete a course of antibiotics I simply take plenty of probiotics and eat a diet rich in fermented foods to re-culture my microbiome. Thankfully none of the children have required any antibiotics thus far.

If a more holistic approach to health is a bit daunting for you, my suggestion is to establish a relationship with a pediatrician, a naturopath (a holistic doctor), and a chiropractor. Utilizing the knowledge of all three professionals will give you a well-rounded view of health and wellness. We tend to go to the chiropractor first, which typically solves any health issues through body alignment and adjustments. Second is our naturopath, and we use our pediatrician last, as we are aware that their approach will be more medicinal than holistic. There is always a place for medicine, however, and we are sure to establish care and create a good relationship with a family doctor wherever we live in case we are ever in need of his or her services.

Fever Reducers

I grew up in an era when fevers were feared, considered dangerous, and usually treated with a reducer of some type. Fevers are a normal part of childhood development and still serve their purpose in adulthood. Fevers fight infection by producing more white blood cells, antibodies, and a group of proteins called interferons, which are known to prevent viral replication and inhibit the growth of cancer cells.[30] Since illness-causing microbes tend to flourish at the body's standard 98.6°, a fever prevents the microbes from reproducing.[31]

Running a fever is not comfortable, but artificially lowering it prompts the body to feel as if it can be more active than it

FEVER

The following concerns should be addressed immediately with fevers:

- The child is under three months old
- No urination within eight hours
- Any fever over 103°
- Listless body after the fever has subsided
- Recurring fever for more than three days

should be, which prolongs the illness. Use wisdom and discernment along with counsel from your pediatrician, naturopath, and/or chiropractor when considering treatment. Most fevers in our household run their course naturally. There have been a few times when we have used a synthetic fever reducer/pain reducer so the body could heal better. Since sleep is so essential to the healing process, if the fever prevents our child from sleeping well, we will give them a small dose of dye-free children's Motrin in order to provide them with a good night's sleep.

I would caution against any use of acetaminophen, however. More and more studies are coming out over the danger of acetaminophen.[32] It is currently the most common cause for acute liver failure in the US.[33] It also tends to deplete the glutathione that naturally presides in the body to fight off free radicals and toxins, leaving the body less armed to fight other illnesses or autoimmune diseases.[34]

Unfortunately, I did not have access to this information on acetaminophen when I first became a mother. We gave Tylenol to our firstborn during teething and for vaccine reactions.

One of the hardest aspects of discovering new and beneficial information is the guilt that comes with knowing you could have done something different, but throughout the years, I have learned to let go of that guilt. My oldest son has some neurological challenges, and while I am not suggesting that Tylenol or vaccines caused these challenges (goodness, I have a whole list of toxic items he was exposed to that I was unaware of at the time), I do know that some children are genetically predisposed to an array of disorders or autoimmune diseases, and certain toxins, allergens, or chemicals can be triggers for their systems.

Since then, we have had all five children genetically tested and have researched the best way to meet their nutritional needs based on what their bodies can or cannot process efficiently, and we have tried to remove most glutathione-depleting foods and toxins in our home. My younger four have benefited from such research and have vastly different immune systems and neurologic responses than my oldest son does, even with sharing some of the same genetic mutations. We have our own little control group in our home, and if I didn't have the ability to compare, I wouldn't be writing this chapter.

Take Heart

Researching health and wellness can be overwhelming, but let me encourage you: you cannot learn it all at once. Through trial and error, you will gain wisdom and understanding of how the body works and responds. It's an ongoing journey, one that I'm sure we'll be on for many more years. Through years of experiencing infections and viruses, you will learn the best methods for treating them, and you will come to understand your child's needs and temperament when it comes to illness.

What works for our family may not work for yours, which is why I remind you again to have a team of health professionals available to help you navigate your way through illness. Many viruses are a normal part of childhood. Rather than fearing them, learn about them through research and information. The more you learn about childhood illnesses, the more you come to understand the immune system and the way the body works.

One of the hard lessons I had to learn and am continually reminded of is that we cannot control everything environmentally, nor do we know the inner workings of each of our family members' bodies. You may be able to keep your family's food clean, but perhaps you live in a heavily polluted area, or maybe you have been able to get rid of every chemical cleaner, but your husband works with toxic materials. We cannot control it all, nor are we created to do so.

Second Peter 1:5–7 says,

> For this very reason, make every effort to supplement your faith with virtue, virtue with knowledge, and knowledge with self-control, and self-control with steadfastness, and steadfastness with godliness, and godliness with brotherly affection, and brotherly affection with love.

In these verses, the Greek word translated as knowledge (*gnōsis*) refers to intellectual knowledge, or awareness. Therefore we know that we are charged to seek information. But when we read the passage in its entirety, we can see we are also called to more than just acquiring knowledge. We must practice virtue, self-control, steadfastness, and godliness. When pursuing a life of holiness, one form of virtue will not dominate the others. In fact, the word translated self-control (*egkrateia*) refs to controlling one's emotions or passions. I know that, at times, I was so intrigued with health and wellness, with figuring out what caused my son's neurological issues, and with questioning the intent of some pharmaceuticals that it became an obsession, and my passion was not controlled.

Thank God for his grace and mercy and for the Holy Spirit who prompts us to keep in step with him, because since then, I have learned to have a balanced approach to health and wellness, to understand that others may not view prevention or treatment the same way I do, and to keep my eyes on Jesus through it all, because not even death will separate us from the love of God.

> For I am sure that neither death nor life, nor angels nor rulers, nor things present nor things to come, nor powers, nor height nor depth, nor anything else in all creation, will be able to separate us from the love of God in Christ Jesus our Lord. (Rom. 8:38–39)

FOR FURTHER READING

Ancient Remedies by Dr. Josh Axe

The Complete Book of Essential Oils and Aromatherapy by Valerie Ann Worwood

Oil Pulling Therapy by Bruce Fife

Earthing: The Most Important Health Discovery Ever! by Clinton Ober

The Vaccine Book by Robert W. Sears

Miller's Review of Critical Vaccine Studies by Neil Miller

WHOLE SPIRITS

8

BIBLICALLY GROUNDED

From childhood you have been acquainted with the sacred writings, which are able to make you wise for salvation through faith in Christ Jesus. All Scripture is breathed out by God and profitable for teaching, for reproof, for correction, and for training in righteousness, that the man of God may be complete, equipped for every good work.

2 Timothy 3:15–17

On one of our first out-of-town trips as new parents, Jason and I visited some of his old high school friends, a married couple who already had three children. As I sat holding my firstborn infant, I asked her what her favorite parenting book was. She responded quickly, "The Bible." I chuckled a little bit because, to be honest, I thought she was joking. The Bible doesn't teach about sleep patterns, discipline techniques, or developmental needs! I changed the subject when I realized she was serious. It took me several years to understand the truth of her response. The Bible is the best parenting book out there, and the only way I was ever going to understand her statement was by discovering the depths of the wisdom and knowledge of God myself.

In Matthew 7, Jesus closes his Sermon on the Mount by saying, "Everyone then who hears these words of mine and does them will be like a wise man who built his house on the rock" (v. 24). In that moment, Jesus drew a line between himself and any other type of religious establishment. His life and his words are the rock upon which we stand; "all other ground is sinking sand," as the old hymn tells us.[1] The more we come to understand the Word of God, the more capable we are of making wise decisions. Not every parenting problem will have a solution in the Bible, but if we keep in step with the Spirit (Gal. 5:16–24), we can rely on God's Word to help guide us individually, so that we can then help guide the precious gifts we were given.

Children in the Word

It is never too early to introduce your children to the Word of God. When they can see it is an essential part of your day, why not make it an essential part of theirs too? When our children were young, we started reading Bible stories using *Egermeier's Bible Story Book* by Elsie Egermeier every morning.[2] What I love about this specific Bible book is its scriptural accuracy and beautiful and timeless illustrations. Sometimes children's books or devotionals "dumb down" the Scriptures in order to appeal to children; however, I found that even my youngest toddlers could understand portions of the stories. After reading the story, I'd ask the kids to tell the story back to me. This always gave me a gauge for what they received from it and what appealed to them. As the older children grew in literacy, I would assign them the task of cross-referencing to assure that the story aligned with the Bible. They would then read aloud the Scripture passage the story was based on, finding out that the stories were almost always word for word. This helped my older children sharpen their oral reading skills and taught them how to cross-reference study materials with Scripture.

One of the benefits of reading Bible stories together is that the stories are relatable for children. They can picture themselves as biblical characters such as Esther, Joshua, or David. One of my favorite stories for children is the story of David and Goliath. I want to raise children who are bold and know who they are in Christ. David's tale of killing Goliath is such a simple story of faith that even a young child can understand it and be stirred to do bold things for God. Every time we read it, we discuss some additional points. For example, although David killed Goliath out of faith in God, he had a reason to trust in God, because before David stood up to Goliath, God had delivered him from a lion and from bears. He knew he could trust in God because he had experience to pull from, and he told King Saul, "The LORD who delivered me from the paw of the lion and from the paw of the bear will deliver me from the hand of this Philistine" (1 Sam. 17:37). Whenever the children are faced with a difficult task, even if it's as simple as a sports tryout or a difficult hike, we remind them that David was empowered by God to do hard things, and God spared him from death each time, even when facing a giant.

Once our children were reading, we established a quiet time of Bible reading and journaling. We call it one of our daily disciplines. Each child has a specific reading plan of their choice. Some have chosen to read the Bible in a year, so they have a daily portion of the New Testament, Old Testament, Proverbs, and Psalms. Others read from the Old Testament to the New Testament. Whatever their plan is, they read for twenty to thirty minutes, and they keep a highlighter and pencil handy to underline or make notes with. At the end of their reading, they select a specific verse that stands out to them and document it in their journal. They also write out a prayer request and something they are grateful for or a testimony of an answered prayer. Since we homeschool, we are able to gather together as a group for our core reading aloud time. During this time, which we have named "morning collective," we each discuss our quiet times. Sometimes there will be a lot of questions about the Scripture passage they read, and other times they will share a Bible story or parable they found helpful or could relate to.

During our morning collective, we also read our Proverbs chapter of the day. Since there are thirty-one Proverbs, it's a great system. One of the children will read the chapter that matches the calendar date. We all read along silently with the assignee and discuss our favorite verse or instruction afterward.

Using the Word to parent my children was a big goal of mine, but I never had the discipline to memorize Scripture in my quiet time. However, when we started homeschooling, I incorporated Scripture memorization into our morning collective so that the kids could learn alongside me. Often I would assess what was going on in our household relationally or with individual kids and then select our weekly verse or verses based on that. For example, if the children had a difficult week getting along, we would memorize Hebrews 12:14: "Strive for peace with everyone, and for the holiness without which no one will see the Lord." One week a specific child was feeling a little insecure, so we memorized Ephesians 2:10: "For we are his workmanship, created in Christ Jesus for good works, which God prepared beforehand, that we should walk in them."

Memorizing Scripture with our children has been one of our greatest tools in stewarding their hearts. Rather than me always acting as the authority figure, we are using the authoritative Word of God—together—to help navigate life. We discovered that turning Scripture into songs by adding our own melodies made it much easier to memorize, and the verses tended to stay on the forefront of our minds. It's also nearly impossible not to join in if someone is singing one. Sometimes, when I can hear the children bickering, I don't intervene but just start singing one of our verses, such as "Beloved, let us love one another, for love is from God, and whoever loves has been born of God and knows God, 1 John 4:7." By the time I'm in the middle of the verse, the children have joined the song, and it redirects the squabble.

Of course this doesn't happen every time, but it's amazing how effective a verse set to song can be in a multitude of situations. In fact, we started selling some of our recorded verses on my homeschooling resource website because they were so helpful. I love to receive feedback from other families that are using God's Word in the same way. It just clarifies the importance and benefits of using Scripture in the home.

We have many stories of moments where we have experienced the fruit of having God's Word written on our hearts. One time there was a downpour of snow as we were driving home from a ski day. It was nearly impossible to see out the window, and the driving conditions were poor. I have one child who tends to get a little anxious with unpredictable situations, so we started singing John 14:27 in as many different tunes as we could come up with: "Peace I leave with you; my peace I give to you. Not as the world gives do I give to you. Let not your hearts be troubled, neither let them be afraid." It effectively diffused the emotions of fear and uncertainty in the car. I didn't need to lecture the child on not being afraid. The verse simply reminded everyone in the car, including me, that there was no reason for our hearts to be troubled.

The beauty of memorizing Scripture is that you can then use it to encourage others. I can't tell you how many times I have been able to pray with someone and have had the authority of God's Word at the tip of my tongue to encourage and remind them of God's promises, although sometimes it's very difficult to share the Scripture without singing it!

The Word of Our Testimony

Horatio G. Spafford was a prominent businessman in the late 1800s in the booming city of Chicago. He was a devout Christian who happened to be close friends with the world-famous evangelist Dwight L. Moody. Horatio and his wife, Anna, had five children, and when their only son died of scarlet fever, the family was devastated. Then, one year later, the Great Chicago Fire destroyed nearly all of their properties. Even in their loss, Horatio and Anna helped others who were grief-stricken and homeless. Two years later, in 1873, they planned a trip to England to visit Moody on one of his speaking events. Horatio had some business to take care of and decided to send his wife and girls ahead of him. While crossing the Atlantic, their steamship was struck by an iron sailing ship, causing it to sink within minutes and taking the lives of two hundred and twenty-six people. Horatio and Anna's four daughters were among those who didn't survive. Anna was later found unconscious off the coast of Cardiff, South Wales, floating on some driftwood. She sent a quick telegram to Horatio as soon as she could, saying, "Saved alone." Horatio immediately set off to be with his wife. At one point in the voyage, the captain summoned Horatio to tell him they were sailing over the location his daughters had died. It is there Horatio wrote the hymn "It Is Well with My Soul."[3]

Part of equipping our children's hearts and spirits to be strong in faith is sharing the testimonies of others and reminding them of our own testimony. Revelation 12:11 says, "And they have conquered him by the blood of the Lamb and by the word of their testimony, for they loved not their lives even unto death." There will be times in their lives where the weight of the world will feel incredibly heavy, but we can remind our children of different testimonies that can encourage them to hold fast to the confession of their hope without wavering, whether the stories are their own experiences or someone else's. Just like Horatio G. Spafford, their spirits can respond to suffering by saying, "Whatever my lot, Thou hast taught me to say, 'it is well, it is well, with my soul.'"[4]

In our household, it's important that our children have an expanded worldview. One of the ways we do this is by sharing a daily story of a martyr. It's eye-opening to read about Christians who do not have the same type of religious freedom we have in America yet choose to live by faith and follow God at all costs. Our society has become so terrified of offense that many children do not know how to stand up for what's right. Reading testimonies of those who stood up for their belief in Christ encourages my children to be bold and to speak the truth.

Some of the books we've read that I would highly recommend are *Foxe's Book of Martyrs* and *Jesus Freaks* volumes 1 and 2. The stories of martyrs they discuss can date back as far as the early church or can be more recent, highlighting stories of modern believers living in countries where there is persecution. My children have learned so much and have been so incredibly stirred and humbled by such stories that they always beg for another. Some of the children have developed a heart for those persecuted in other countries and will often journal prayers for them. While these aren't your typical feel-good stories, they are testimonies that build faith and courage and provide a sobering perspective for what is going on in other countries, while also reminding each of us that "to live is Christ, and to die is gain" (Phil. 1:21). We have had a lot of difficult, deep conversations regarding martyrdom, because reading such stories causes us to question what we would do in the same situation. It provides us with the opportunity to do a heart check to see if our priorities are that of the world or if they are eternal.

We also take any opportunity to share a personal testimony we have experienced or have heard from a friend in order to help our children understand God's faithfulness. For example, there were two different couples in our church that were having a hard time conceiving a baby. We asked them individually if they would allow our family to pray with them. Each of our children laid hands on them and prayed for God to provide them with their own families. When we found out that both of the couples were expecting, we celebrated by hooting and hollering and thanking God for the miracle of life. Both couples now have multiple children, and we find the news just as exciting with every new pregnancy, because our children know that their prayers were heard, and they have yet another story to add to their personal testimony of God's faithfulness. Anytime we experience a crisis or trial in our family, we walk through our many stories of God's faithfulness as a reminder, just as Scripture tells us to do: "We will not hide them from their children, but tell to the coming generation the glorious deeds of the LORD, and his might, and the wonders that he has done" (Ps. 78:4).

When our twins were two years old, Jason was unemployed for nearly a year. That was one of the most faith-building years we have had in our family. Jason was able to be in the Word and in prayer for hours each day, and the Lord led us so faithfully through what felt like a financial wilderness. While we were going through this time, we asked the Lord to keep us out of debt and to allow us to continue to eat healthy foods. Our grocery budget didn't change, and yet he provided every need. Several times, just when the mortgage was due, I would get a photography job that would cover it. Our local co-op traded me groceries for some photography and marketing work for a period of time. One day, we were completely out of money and needed to pay our electrical bill, and Jason asked the kids to help scavenge for quarters and change throughout the house so that we could pay it. They happily went around the house searching for anything they could find, and by the time we emptied our various change jars, we were able to fully pay the bill.

After eight months of unemployment, we found ourselves, again, completely out of money. I remember coming in from a run and Jason handing me an envelope to open. There was a beautifully written letter from a stranger who expressed her appreciation for my willingness to share our journey of following Christ on my blog. As I finished reading, I noticed a cashier's check for a substantial amount of money was included in the back. When I saw the check, I fell to my knees out of awe and gratefulness. Only God could have orchestrated such timing and planted that in her heart! We didn't know it at the time, but that check would turn out to be just the right amount of money to last us until Jason's first paycheck from his new job.

When Jason found himself unemployed again just recently, due to COVID-19, we had our many stories of how God had been faithful to us in the past to encourage us. The second time, it didn't feel as scary or as unknown. One evening, as Jason was asking each of us to share a story from the past where God provided, our oldest son, Carter, mentioned his memory of gathering coins to pay the electric bill. Though he was only eight at the time, he remembered! He remembered God's faithfulness and had that story as his own to pull from. I didn't realize how much the children were aware of during that first experience of unemployment, but they all had a memory or two from that year, and it was such a blessing to hear them share their hope in God's provision for the season we were about to encounter.

Unbeknownst to us, the same person who was prompted to give us that check the first time played a role in Jason finding a job the second time. I will never be able to understand the plans of God here on earth, but Everett reminded us then that "we know that for those who love God all things work together for good, for those who are called according to his purpose" (Rom. 8:28). Practicing the habit of remembering and sharing our testimony continually with our children helps them develop an understanding of God's nature and brings comfort and confidence in times of hardship.

9

SERVICE

> For you were called to freedom, brothers. Only do not use your freedom as an opportunity for the flesh, but through love serve one another.
>
> Galatians 5:13

I am confident that I do not have the gift of serving or hospitality. Both acts are something I have always struggled with, as they are not my natural instinct, nor am I completely comfortable with either. Jason took me to a family holiday gathering shortly after we started dating. I was astounded at how many people there were. Dozens of family, friends, and even acquaintances who didn't have somewhere else to go for the holiday all showed up to spend time with one another and eat delicious food. I watched as his mother effortlessly set the table, chopped vegetables, and prepared a large meal for so many. It was incredibly admirable, and to this day it is evident that serving and hospitality are both gifts she possesses.

After the meal was served, Jason hopped out of his chair and started clearing plates, washing dishes, and tidying up. To see the both of them serve so generously while others (including myself) sat around sipping tea and eating dessert was inspiring and, to be honest, a bit convicting. Because Jason's parents were such great models for serving and hospitality, Jason learned by example and by that same method has now taught me and our children what it means to serve others.

Serving Opportunities

One of the things I've learned from being married to someone with the gift of serving is that they are always looking for serving opportunities. Jason truly lives a life in line with Philippians 2:4, "Let each of you look not only to his own interests, but also to the interests of others." If anyone has a need and he hears about it, you can guarantee he will drop everything he has planned for the day to help. It's beautiful to watch him serve so wholeheartedly.

From the time the children were small, even when the twins were babies, Jason involved them in any type of serving. We believed that just because they were little didn't mean they couldn't bless people. Even if it took them an entire day filled with water and potty breaks, and all they achieved was raking one corner of a lawn, they were there serving, and it brought joy to those they were helping, to us, and most importantly, to the Lord. Because we started the children so young, they have learned that serving comes with being a part of our family. It's not a chore or a task but an opportunity to show God's love to those who need it (Heb. 13:16).

Serving looks different in every situation. Our boys are now expert movers, as we have helped many people pack up their homes and load moving trucks. Scarlett and I have helped clean out homes, unpack, and paint for those who need it. We have served in soup kitchens and volunteered in church outreaches. But for the most part, serving opportunities usually look like helping a neighbor catch up on their weeding or lawn care, last-minute babysitting, providing a meal for a family in crisis, or cutting and stacking wood for a single mom.

Even though we have done these things as a family, and Jason loves to jump at any opportunity, I want to be candid that serving is not always easy for everyone involved. We have watched who gets easily motivated by serving and who needs extra motivation. It's usually me and maybe one other child who need that extra motivation! Of course we all feel great afterward, but in my flesh, it's a struggle I have to overcome for the sake of loving our neighbors and enabling Jason to work in his gifting. As writer and speaker Jackie Hill Perry once tweeted, "You don't have to feel obedient to be obedient."[1] Many times I work through this struggle in our serving ventures, and I often have to remind myself (and any child struggling with giving up their Saturday) that it's an act of obedience. When we are done with serving, we'll do something special as a family, like get ice cream or watch a family movie that evening as a thank-you to our children for selflessly spending their time meeting the needs of others.

One of the things I have noticed with serving is that usually the same people show up every time. Based on experience, I think it is likely someone in the family has the deep desire to help and wants to take their other family members along, a lot like Jason and me. I have seen these families throughout the years show up consistently, with willing hearts and joyful spirits. Often we were the youngest family participating, so my children were able to watch older kids work hard for someone else, without any personal earthly gain. I am so grateful to have been a part of many situations where these older kids modeled such behavior. Whenever we get in the car to leave, Jason and I always highlight the actions of the other families, recognizing their work ethic and heart posture while serving. This teaches our children how to respond and how to work, without us lecturing or explaining the importance of it. Now that our children are older, they are the examples for other younger kids to look up to, and there is something so beautiful about experiencing this full circle together.

Serving the Family

We have a few different systems that help keep our household functioning efficiently. From the time our children could walk, they had specific assignments and household duties. If children are old enough to understand and obey, they are old enough to start chores or duties. The earlier a child understands that they are not just a consumer but a contributor, the higher their self-esteem and self-worth are. They also tend to be less selfish and demanding. Yes, we are all born with a sinful and selfish spirit, but the sooner you can equip a child to understand that the world doesn't revolve around them, the better. When a child contributes to the family, they are now a part of a team, and without their help, the household will not function as it should. This gives ownership to the child; they know that without their contribution, the family would suffer.

One day when August, one of the twins, was about two years old, he was wiping off the table after dinner (not perfectly, but the action is more important than ability at that age). Jason came over and placed his hand on August's head and said, "Thank you for serving our family so happily, Gus." I loved the way he phrased that. It was an act of service. Many times, as a stay-at-home mom, I had to remind myself that my job as a wife, mother, homemaker, and teacher was not to serve myself but to serve them. I needed that reminder so much that we memorized Galatians 5:13 together so it would be written on my heart: "For you were called to freedom, brothers. Only do not use your freedom as an opportunity for the flesh, but through love serve one another." Ever since that day, we have thanked our children for serving their family as they do their chores and duties.

I have gotten a lot of inquiries throughout the years from mothers in the early stages of parenting who are trying to figure out what their family stance is on chores, allowance, and requirements for children. I am happy to share what we have done in the past as well as our perspective behind some of our decisions below.

Our children started with small tasks from the moment they could walk. Having the children so close together in age, I was able to see how much children are capable of and at what age certain duties could be started. Keep in mind, as these are listed, that the ability to finish the job adequately grows as they develop. A two-year-old should not be expected to perfectly wipe the table, scrub the stains, and rinse out the rag. But they can wet the rag, wipe the table in sweeping motions, and shake the rag out into the trash. You may find morsels around the trashcan as well as some still on the table, but at that age, they don't have the dexterity to be able to execute perfectly. The same goes for a nine-year-old scrubbing the toilet or a ten-year-old ironing a shirt. Pay attention to their growth and ability, as they develop quickly and will need some accountability on the tasks they are required to complete.

CHORES BY AGE

Toddler Years (Ages 2–4)

Wiping the table and countertops

Unloading the dishwasher into lower cabinets

Organizing the silverware drawer

Dusting

Sorting laundry and matching socks

Picking up yard debris

Watering outdoor plants

Younger Child (Ages 5–8)

Cleaning windows

Vacuuming

Sweeping

Cleaning out the car

Organizing

Folding laundry

Stacking wood

Feeding and watering animals

Unloading and putting away groceries

Wiping cabinets

Watering indoor plants

Older Child (Ages 9–12)

Maintaining fire in woodstove

Shoveling snow

Running loads of laundry

Cleaning bathrooms

Changing sheets

Doing dishes

Mowing lawns / doing yard work

Mopping

Doing trash duty

Cleaning the refrigerator

Washing vehicles

My children may be older now, but I do not forget the amount of effort it took to teach them these skills. I understand it is much easier to do such tasks on your own, as you often have to follow up after the child in order for the job to be done thoroughly. However, the time put in during those early years will not go to waste. You are investing in your household. The more effort you put in during the early years, the more rewards you will experience in the later years. Some rewards are physical, such as a clean house and car, but other rewards are long-term, such as establishing a strong work ethic in your children, ensuring a lack of entitlement and an understanding of how a household operates, and numerous skills that can translate to finding a good job. My goal is that by the time my children reach their teens, they are able to adequately execute all of these duties correctly and thoroughly.

We also have categories for tasks and duties in our family to help define some of the expectations. Having these expectations allows the children to fall into a rhythm and also holds them accountable. We try to keep the expectations consistent for at least a year so they can master their jobs before acquiring more or changing tasks.

Their daily responsibilities are called "daily disciplines." This is a term we use in our homeschooling as well. Daily disciplines are acts done every day to keep things in order and keep their bodies healthy. These include tasks such as running or working out, making the bed, brushing teeth, picking up after oneself, schoolwork, and personal assigned chores. We also have weekly chores, which are usually done on Friday afternoons.

We developed family work day, which is on Saturdays, when the children were very small. Now that their schedules include work and sports, we practice family work day one to three times a month. This is a day where the entire family typically works on house projects and yard maintenance. We usually do something special for lunch or have dessert as a reward for willingly working together.

We have never provided an allowance and don't intend to. I have heard of the benefits of providing one, such as teaching money management or aiding accountability with chores, but for us, we would rather our children be motivated to seek outside money-making opportunities than be paid by their parents. We believe that daily disciplines and weekly chores are a part of contributing to and serving the family and should not be rewarded monetarily. However, that being said, we do provide opportunities for our children to make money in their earlier years, when they are too young to find a job outside the home.

We pay our children for tasks above and beyond what is expected from them. Some of these tasks include weeding and trimming, cleaning out the garage, doing small construction jobs, painting, sanding, and other jobs that come up that are out of the ordinary. We also look for other opportunities for them to work. Grandparents have done a wonderful job employing them for certain tasks, and so have neighbors and friends. The goal is to get them used to working for someone else and to do an efficient job, so that by the time they are ready for the workforce, they are well-equipped and confident in taking orders from an employer.

We also encourage entrepreneurialism. As the saying goes, necessity is the mother of invention. Our hope is that by not providing all of our children's "wants," they will find ways to make the money to fulfill those desires. When they go through dry seasons of finding work, we encourage them to think of ideas that will make money. Like teaching them household chores, this is not done entirely independently. They need help learning to navigate concepts such as profit margins and startup costs. We have partnered with them several times. In some instances they make a fair amount of money, and other times they break even or even lose some, but the point is that they try, and they learn how to start something.

One time our oldest son, Carter, wanted to start a ski tech company. He was frustrated with the amount of money that the ski resort charged for a ski waxing, and he decided he could probably do it more cheaply; he could earn money while also creating an opportunity for others to pay less. We arranged for him to meet with an out-of-town friend who was once the US Ski Team head ski tech. Carter was able to learn how to wax and tech from a professional. He was also taught about the differences in types of waxes. He researched everything he needed in order to start his business. If I remember correctly, the startup cost was around $600. Jason and I thought this was a great opportunity for him to learn how to raise funds. Neither of us invested in his company. We did, however, help him put together a proposal to use when he contacted potential investors. He was twelve at the time. It was an incredible learning experience for him. He raised funds to purchase everything and was able to pay back his partners within the first ski season.

Before you get too impressed, after all of that effort on our end, Carter chose not to run his business the following season. He decided the profit margin was not high enough to justify time spent. We do not consider that a loss but rather a wonderful learning experience. It taught him to calculate time as money and to look for other opportunities that might have lower operating expenses. He also learned that the price of a waxing at the ski resort was definitely justified!

Throughout the years, there have been other businesses such as roadside "thrift stores," lemonade stands, bake sales, concession stands, wildflower bouquet sales, and rehabilitated golf ball sales. Children lose interest quickly, though. Most of the time they will make a nice sum of money, then tire of the work involved to maintain the sales. At first this was frustrating to me, as I could see all of the potential, but I had to remember that they're kids and their attention span is short-sighted. To help keep their entrepreneurial spirit alive, I will assign business books in their school reading, such as *Rich Dad, Poor Dad for Teens* by Robert Kiyosaki, or I will have them take a year off of math in order to go through Dave Ramsey's personal finance course. One of my sons is adamant about not going to college. To be able to provide for his family, he'll need to understand how to run a business and manage finances. Publisher Simply Charlotte Mason provides a "your business math" curriculum that allows a child to own and operate a fictional bookstore or sports store. They learn basic accounting as well as how to forecast seasonal sales, how to manage excess inventory, and much more.[2]

Kingdom Economy

Another reason we choose to invest our time and effort into partnering with our children in learning money skills is so they can learn the biblical perspective on giving. When I was in high school, my dad and I would chat after dinner every night. We would both have a cup of coffee and discuss politics, religion, real estate, and humanity. Those were rich conversations, and

I hold them close to my heart. I didn't know it at the time, but I would lose my dad to brain cancer in my first year of college, making those memories all the more special. I remember one conversation where he told me about my grandfather getting audited by the IRS. Both my grandpa and my dad were pastors, so their income was not substantial. Having the IRS audit my grandpa seemed like a waste of taxpayer dollars. However, my grandfather gave more money away than he made, and his taxes were never balanced because of it—and so he was audited, not once but twice! Even when they tallied his bills, receipts, and pay stubs, they could not figure out how he could give more than he received. I asked my dad, "How was that possible?" His laconic response, accompanied with a large, toothy grin, was, "kingdom economy." The two IRS auditors were equally as dumbfounded, but their visit was not wasted because they both left as new believers. Their experience of kingdom economy was substantial enough to win their hearts for Christ.

Luke 6:38 says, "Give, and it will be given to you. Good measure, pressed down, shaken together, running over, will be put into your lap. For with the measure you use it will be measured back to you." My grandparents' lives were a perfect example of good measure being put into their laps. They never lived lavishly; in fact, I was always so impressed with how humbly they lived, but they were always giving. When it came time for them to sell their home and build a small in-laws quarters on my cousin's property, we watched several contractors and business owners pull together to build them a modest home. Flooring, plumbing, appliances, and roofing—everything was covered by the people my grandparents had given to throughout the years.

When Jason and I bought our quirky 1,200-square-foot house, my grandpa was ninety-six. By this point he was both blind and nearly deaf, but my grandma walked through the fixer-upper with him, narrating her inspection of every corner. He decided we needed some form of air conditioning, as I was pregnant with the twins and the house did not have any. He went out that day (my grandmother drove) and came back with a $500 swamp cooler. We knew they didn't have a lot of money. This gift was beyond what we could accept, so we refused. He put his face very close to mine, grabbed both of my arms, and said, "Jodi, don't you dare take away the blessing of us giving. This is not just for you. The blessing is ours." I was taken aback by the concept. I had never considered the giver's reward in such situations, and the strength of my grandpa's response showed me how denying such a gift would deny their blessing.

From then on, I have viewed giving through such a lens of kingdom economy. Granted, I do not believe that one should give in order to receive. What I do believe, because I have seen the provisional fruit in our own lives and the lives of others such as my grandparents, is that by giving generously and wholeheartedly, you can rely on the fact that you and your family's needs will be met. We have never gone a day without food, and neither have my grandparents. God even tells us to test his provision through tithing by saying, "Bring the full tithe into the storehouse, that there may be food in my house. And thereby put me to the test, says the LORD of hosts, if I will not open the windows of heaven for you and pour down for you a blessing until there is no more need" (Mal. 3:10). This verse was the result of God calling out the people as robbers who had withheld their tithes (vv. 8–9). Theologian R. C. Sproul responds to these verses, saying,

> Malachi's teaching indicates that when we fail to tithe, we are not merely robbing the church, the clergy, or Christian educators—we

are robbing God Himself. But note that God had words not only of condemnation for the people but also a promise of prosperity were they to change their ways. God challenged them to be faithful, giving His own promise that He would open the windows of heaven and pour out blessings upon them.[3]

Tithing is a biblical responsibility and an act of obedience. Include your children in the process. When our children were too young to earn money, they would be the ones to put the folded check in the offering bag, practicing the principle before they fully understood what it meant. Once they started earning money, we taught them to take the first 10 percent before they spent any money and give it to the storehouse. Our storehouse has been different throughout the years. For the most part, we have attended a church and considered that church our storehouse. We are sure to check out the church's finances and allocation of such funds to determine and discern if our tithe should go there. For the most part, we have been very satisfied with how the churches we have attended fed back into the kingdom of God. There was a time when we were a part of a home church, and since it didn't necessarily have any operating expenses or missional projects, we would set aside our full tithe to await opportunities to which we felt led to give. This was such an enjoyable part of tithing because we were involved in passing money through the kingdom of God on a more personal scale.

Invite your children into your giving decisions and help them understand where your firstfruits are going and who they are helping. By doing so, you are modeling a lifestyle of gratitude and faithfulness. When your children start to see how kingdom economy works, they learn to view money as God's and not their own.

10

THE POWER OF WORDS

Death and life are in the power of the tongue, and those who love it will eat its fruits.

Proverbs 18:21

My parents always referred to me as "Joyful Jodi." The words they've spoken over me, from my childhood to this day, are a large part of my identity. Once I started learning about the power of words and the significance of using biblical truths as affirmation, I realized that what they saw in me, their belief in my purpose, and their commitment to speak such words over me helped affirm who I was created to be and shape who I was to become in Christ.

Life or Death

Proverbs 12:18 says, "There is one whose rash words are like sword thrusts, but the tongue of the wise brings healing." There is ample opportunity to either make or break the spirit of our children through the words we use with them in our daily communication. Words have purpose. God spoke the world into existence with words, and we are welcomed into relationship with him through his written Word, the Bible. Words can either edify (give life to) or tear down (bring death to) others by their simple use (18:21). There are various forms of words that can impact the way we view ourselves, how we shape our children, and how we relate to others.

Music, books, and media are ways words come into the home. We are selective about music, making sure that it edifies all who are listening, and we are likewise aware of what books and television we consume. In our homeschooling journey, I have always held fast to the idea that everything we read or listen to should be filled with truth and beauty. This ideal has given us years of beautiful education. The children can quickly identify a book that is poorly written or filled with nonsense versus a book that is well written and contains honorable characters.

We chose not to have a television until our children reached their teen years. We eventually moved into a home with a great place for family movie nights, and we made the big decision to bring a television in. It's a lot easier to control the content being spoken over your children when there is not a television in the home; however, we are selective about what we watch. One of the ongoing tests we use is Luke 6:45: "The good person out of the good treasure of his heart produces good, and the evil person out of his evil treasure produces evil, for out of the abundance of the heart his mouth speaks." We know that if our children take on certain attitudes, tones, or slang that are not appropriate or respectful in our home, they are likely getting it from the television, and we then take extra measures to monitor what's going into their ears and hearts. The same goes for our marriage. We have worked very hard to protect our marriage from messages that are often normalized through television shows and movies regarding morality and marriage, including how married characters speak to their spouses or treat marriage. When we recognize that life or death are the only two possible results from words spoken, then assessing what messages are coming into our spirit becomes an essential part of protecting what goes into the heart.

Just like finding a balanced approach to food, though, we are careful not to get too extreme when it comes to television and music. Our children need to be equipped to be able to make choices for themselves that will edify their spirits, but not out of judgment or legalism. We are still learning what that looks like. I'm not sure if we will ever figure it out, but it is an open conversation that is always on the table. I call this process the "push and pull of parenting," as there is always movement one way or another, whether it's giving more freedom or tightening some family boundaries.

Positive Truths

We can speak over our children with words that make them aware of their identity. As they grow and create their worldview and develop their understanding of who they are in Christ, we have the honor of introducing them to biblical truths that help shape their perspective. Biblical truths are not fluffy, empty praises we shower on our children and hope for the best. They are promises, and through redundantly speaking them to our children, we help them learn to hold on to such words as truth.

I once read about such declarations in Patricia Bootsma's book *Raising Burning Hearts*, and I was encouraged to see that

FAMILY PROCLAMATIONS

You are a "mighty man of valor" and the Lord is with you (Judg. 6:12).

You are the head; you are not the tail (Deut. 28:13).

You are a leader to leaders and a follower of Jesus Christ (Ps. 78:70–72; Phil. 2:12–13).

You are a blessing wherever you go; you are not a burden (Ps. 127:3).

You walk in favor with God and man (Prov. 3:4).

You are bold, and you speak the truth (Eph. 6:19).

You "shall lend to many nations"; you will never borrow (Deut. 15:6).

The fruit of the Spirit lives inside of you (2 Cor. 3:17–18).

God is for you, and you are destined for righteousness (Rom. 8:30–31).

her grown children continued to live out the biblical truths in adulthood she proclaimed over them as children. I've adopted some of the truths she spoke over her children, and we've added some others to create our own family statements as well.

When I speak these truths over my children, they are fully engaged, soak the words in like sponges, and are refreshed by the time I am finished. Even after years of sharing the same statements, they are attentive and responsive to the words. All of my children have memorized them and will often say them along with me. I have also heard them speak the same words over other family members throughout the years, and it blesses me greatly to see them do so.

Sometimes I will speak them all at once, and other times I will single out a statement when it applies to a specific scenario. For example, whenever I am dropping off my children somewhere, I always remind them, "You are a blessing, not a burden." I want to positively remind them they are a blessing but also encourage them to fulfill that truth rather than be a burden. Sometimes when the children are arguing, or when something has happened to expose sin (which happens on the daily), I will remind them, "The fruit of the Spirit lives inside of you." We will discuss what the fruit is and how it wasn't shown. If there is a situation that requires a certain level of courage or bravery, I will remind them, "You are a mighty man (or woman) of valor, and the Lord is with you."

Years ago, the children and I were working through a study of Africa. After weeks of learning about some of its different countries, including economies and history, we decided to pool our money together to buy some goats for a family in Tanzania and to sponsor a child in Uganda. My oldest son, Carter, was ten at the time. Once we had selected a child, he kept studying her profile and said, "We are lending to many nations, Mom!" It was a beautiful moment as he was able to fully comprehend some of the truths spoken over him daily.

One day, I picked up Scarlett from a sports event and we started up a conversation about some girls on her team. She mentioned that a few of the girls were very cruel to each other, and it made her uncomfortable to hang out with them when they treated each other that way. I asked her what she did about it. She said that she told them it was hard for her to listen to them treat each other that way. Scarlett is my most introverted and quiet child, so it came as a shock to me that she spoke out. I said, "Wow, that was bold!" She responded, "I spoke the truth!"

Everett was born with an intense desire to work with his hands, hunt, and fish. Since neither Jason nor I have much experience with hunting, we prayed diligently for someone to come into his life who would be willing to teach him. After a few months of daily prayer over Everett's needs and desires, Jason ran into a new neighbor and introduced himself. Within minutes he found out that this neighbor was extremely passionate about the same things as Everett and had also mentored a few kids throughout the years who shared his passion. It was such a divine conversation, but we also didn't want to put all of our hope in our neighbor. A few days later, however, he called us with an offer to take Everett boar hunting. We all took a moment to thank God for his provision and to recognize Everett's "favor with God and man." He was able to develop a relationship with this mentor and go on hunting trips with him as well. Jason and I were so grateful, as our prayers were answered and God's favor was so evident.

It is important to recognize when these truths come to fruition. Discuss the situations as a family and thank the Lord together for his provision and favor. Each time you recognize the promises of God unfolding, your children increase in the knowledge of his sovereign, loving, and fatherly nature, and they are able to apply those experiences to their understanding of who they are in Christ.

One thing our family has learned throughout the past few years, though, is that recognizing these truths does not always have to come about through something positive. God is not just a God of provision, and our relationship shouldn't just be based on his favor. He is also the God of comfort (2 Cor. 1:3). When we face difficult times, we need to rest in the fact that he is our refuge and our strength, an ever-present help in times of trouble (Ps. 46:1). Our family's faith has grown far deeper in times of sorrow and suffering than it ever has in times of provision.

When COVID-19 broke out in March 2020, Jason lost his job immediately. We were unsure how long it would take for him to find a new job, so after much prayer, we decided to sell our house to buy some time. The decision to sell was one of the most difficult decisions we have ever faced. The home itself was just a house, but the circumstances that surrounded it were very fragile.

Our extended family owned the property around and across from it, and selling felt like the death of a lifelong dream. By selling we were also taking a big risk ourselves, hurting family, and leaving an idyllic setting for our own children. Breaking the news to our family and children was heartbreaking, and the months that followed were filled with more sorrow and loss. Our beloved dog got attacked, recovered, but then got hit by a car and died. I was a witness in a sexual abuse case, and our church was in shambles as a result of it. We lost many friends through the process, and it was easily the most devastating year of our lives. However, Jason is a mighty man of valor, and the Lord was with us all the way. Jason beautifully led our family every night through stories of miracles and provision we had experienced in our family. Every night the children were excited to share a memory of God's provision or comfort. Those stories, like the twelve stones of memorial in Joshua 4, reminded us of God's goodness. We knew that he would guide us through, because we had story after story to fall back on in remembrance.

The words spoken every night at our table were the testimony we relied on, knowing our faith and our Father would guide us and care for us no matter where we lived.

Speaking truth over your children also helps in other forms of parenting, as it brings you back to the Word each time there is conflict or confusion in decision-making. Just because we speak positive truths in our children's lives does not mean they'll always make correct choices or have conflict-free relationships. Using these truths as a tool and reminder is a way to bring their flesh back to focusing on their identity in Christ, just as we do in our personal walk.

Cultivating an Encouraging Atmosphere in the Home

We practice a few habits and traditions in our home that encourage an atmosphere of positivity. Because daily life tends to be consumed with correcting hearts, working through disputes, and promoting accountability for personal tasks and chores, we try to take advantage of times when there are opportunities to connect as a family over something positive.

One of these traditions is birthday affirmations. Each family member gets the opportunity to pick a special "birthday cereal" the day before their birthday. On the morning of, we gather together and consume copious amounts of corn syrup and food coloring. As we sit around the table, it's a tradition for each person to say two things they love about the birthday boy or girl. It has to be personal, specific, and something only a close friend or family member would know. The deposit placed in their spirit is so substantial, you can witness the joy and appreciation on their faces.

Another habit both Jason and I try to practice is to uplift each other in front of our children. My father was a pastor, and because of the constant needs in the church, we had an answering machine that screened all incoming phone calls. I can remember every weeknight, before he came home from work, he would call and leave us a message, saying, "My precious family! I cannot wait to come home to you. My beloved wife, I will be home soon!" I can remember the feeling I had as a young girl every time he called. I felt cherished, and I knew he wanted to spend time with me.

I shared those memories with Jason just months into our marriage. Bless him and his heart because he began doing the same thing. We may not have an answering machine, but he will text or call. When he returns home from work, he will make sure everyone knows just how grateful he is to be home and to be with us. He also has taught me so much about lifting up each other in front of the children. Jason is always boasting about me to our children or in front of our friends. It's not an over-the-top exaggeration; he simply finds ways to build me up in normal conversation. From his example, I have learned to do the same, even though it does not come completely naturally to me. When I share positive things about him in front of our children or our friends, he feels honored and appreciated.

One of our practices is to thank Jason, our main provider, for all of his hard work anytime we are able to go out to a restaurant. Instead of thanking me for the delicious dinner, which happens when we eat at home, the children and I thank him for all of the hard work he has done in order to take us to dinner. One time, Jason took a few of our boys to meet up with a friend for dinner. When they were finished, the friend decided to pay for everyone. The boys immediately thanked him for working so hard to pay for their meal. His friend was taken aback and told Jason that the gesture blessed him and made him feel appreciated. It's a small practice, but it's a substantial way to speak life into family members or friends and a habit that will hopefully be brought into their own homes one day.

Also, there are certain phrases I use with the children that are meant to help diffuse emotional responses to normal situations. Most of the tension within our home is between siblings, so it has been a fine line to navigate between letting them work things out on their own and knowing when to jump in and help with conflict resolution. Here are a few questions I ask the children, depending on the situation:

"Are you helping or hurting?"
"Are you encouraging or discouraging?"
"Are you speaking life or death?"

Children (and adults) will go pretty far to justify their actions and words when they are hurt or angry. The above questions have helped stop the process of defending their actions and placed the responsibility on their heart posture.

We have a lot of parenting ahead, and we are no experts, but our experience with witnessing the power of words and how they can be used to speak life, truth, and love to our children has given enough fruit for us to keep going—and to continue for generations. Anytime my children are with my mom or on the phone with her, she will ask them, "What are you to Grammy and Opa?" They respond, "A joy and a blessing." She obviously taught them that, but it encourages me so much to see how grandparents can encourage and speak life into their grandchildren. I hope to speak the same biblical truths that we have practiced with our own children over our future grandchildren. "So even to old age and gray hairs, O God, do not forsake me, until I proclaim your might to another generation, your power to all those to come" (Ps. 71:18).

11

SPIRIT LED

I tell you the truth: it is to your advantage that I go away, for if I do not go away, the Helper will not come to you. But if I go, I will send him to you.

John 16:7

After forty-plus years of life, I can share story after story of how the quiet quickening of the Holy Spirit has helped lead our family. These stories and outcomes have strengthened our faith and grown our understanding of the divine Trinity. Raised in a charismatic church, home, and school, I never questioned the Holy Spirit's presence in my life. However, as I matured, I came to realize that my understanding of the gospel was a little lopsided. This was not due to my upbringing or denomination but mostly to my lack of time in God's Word. As I began to dive deep into Scripture, and continue to do so, I am comforted in knowing that the Holy Spirit is alive and active, and that his voice has led me through many situations in the past.

Based on my experience, and talking to many other believers throughout the years, I think that how we are raised or introduced to Christ can affect how we view the Holy Spirit's role in our lives, and sometimes we are confused or misled. Either we become Spirit dependent, like I was, or we're overly concerned or skeptical about the biblical purpose of the Spirit, therefore seeing him as less than what the Bible declares. However, in John 14, Jesus clearly speaks of God his Father sending a Helper, the Holy Spirit, who will "teach [us] all things and bring to [our] remembrance all that [Jesus has] said to [us]" (v. 26).

The Bible tells us that, from the beginning, the Holy Spirit was active. Genesis 1:2 states that the Spirit of God "[hovered] over the face of the deep." In 2 Timothy 3:16 we are told that "all Scripture is breathed out by God," and Peter affirms this view by writing, "No prophecy was ever produced by the will of man, but men spoke from God as they were carried along by the Holy Spirit" (2 Pet. 1:21). Therefore, we can trust, since the Holy Spirit is equal to God and Jesus, and they are all one, that what he has to say is true. However, we are told to test spirits in 1 John 4:1–2. Because his voice is often quiet (1 Kings 19:12), it can be difficult to discern whether what we're hearing is imagined or from our sovereign God. There are a few questions I have learned to ask to identify the source of the quiet voice:

Is this in line with the Word of God and God's character?
Does this message encourage the fruit of the Spirit in me?
Does this produce peace or further understanding?

Asking those three questions helps me determine whether or not the Holy Spirit is speaking to me. Another way to test the spirit is to look at past situations when I heard a quiet voice and determine whether that voice led to peace or destruction. Remembering the past is a significant way to acknowledge the power of God or recognize times when I have leaned on my own understanding.

There are many ways the Holy Spirit has taught us and helped us, as well as ways we teach our children the correct understanding of God and the divine Trinity.

Parenting

When the children were small and my only daily break was a forty-five-minute run, I would use that time to pray over them, praise God, and also seek understanding or help. My run became a special time between me and the Lord, and I received so much guidance throughout the years during that time. Once the children were older and able to be home alone or were more self-sufficient, quiet times became easier and longer, but during the years of sleep deprivation and baby food making, my daily run was my time for undivided attention on God.

Years ago, Jason and I were living in a temporary rental with our then-three children: Carter, age four, Everett, age two, and baby Scarlett. Everett started waking up at five o'clock and would climb into bed with me. Jason and I had decided we would not co-sleep, but part of my heart sympathized with my two-year-old. We had moved and had recently had a baby, and Jason was gone four days a week, so perhaps Everett was sorting through some emotions and needed some cuddle time with his mom. However, I was very tired due to nursing my newborn baby in the night, and five o'clock was not the time I was hoping to give him cuddles. After three days of this pattern, I humbly, almost shamefully, asked God for help while I was on my daily run. I remember saying something along the lines of, "Lord, I know this is so silly, but I want to do the right thing as a mother, both for me and for him. Is this a discipline issue, or is it a need of his that I should be meeting?" I heard a gentle voice say, *This is a discipline issue.* Immediately I felt a peace that I wasn't expecting.

I was so confident this response was the voice of the Spirit that I told Everett that night, "Everett, it is not acceptable for you to be getting up at five. You may not get up until the sun comes through your window. If you do, there will be consequences." Sure enough, Everett got up at five o'clock the next morning, and I had to follow through with his consequences. I also found pockets of time throughout that day to love on him individually and make sure his needs of physical affection were met. When I woke up the following morning, I remember seeing the sun shining through the window, which meant that Everett had not gotten up at five. I lay there smiling over a good night's sleep, and I thanked the Lord for caring for something as small as a young mother's sleep and the character of her two-year-old child. Everett and I made pancakes that morning, and while he doesn't remember that situation, it's a simple story of God's faithfulness that has been written on my heart.

This experience may seem insignificant to you, but when you begin to understand the nature of God, you begin to converse with him as you would a friend (John 15:15). I wouldn't withhold questions about my toddler's discipline issues or concerns about my child's behavior from a good friend, so why would I from God? I got in a habit of pouring my heart out to him. I talk to him about marriage, friendships, parenting, and more. Does that mean he responds every time with a clear answer or direction? Not at all. But there are certainly memorable times I've experienced great confidence in his voice, whether through his providing an answer, direction, or encouragement or even prompting me to make changes in my life.

Another example of the Holy Spirit prompting me is a redemptive story of attachment with my daughter, Scarlett. Scarlett (whom we lovingly call Lulu) was only a year old when we found out I was pregnant with the twins. The twins' pregnancy was incredibly intense, and for the first few months I could barely get off the couch. Jason would bring fried eggs to me at 4:00 a.m. in order for me to be able to get out of bed. I threw up every time I ate, and my body was exhausted. Lulu was already an independent baby, and I remember lying on the couch with her playing on the floor with Everett for hours. I was so grateful that she didn't need me because I had nothing to give. It breaks my heart to write these words and to picture her little blond head as she played independently. After the twins were born, her independence was a continued gift, because rather than lying on the couch, I was nursing and diapering two babies all day long. Jason's job demanded a lot of time from him, so I was spending long days and evenings taking care of the needs of my five babies alone. Lulu was such a gift and a blessing, helping with the babies' clothes, toys, and diapers and entertaining herself while I cared for her tiny brothers.

When the twins eventually made it through the infancy phase, and they became less reliant on me, I began to notice that Lulu didn't need me in any way. She didn't come to me when she was hurt, she didn't need affection, and she rarely sought either of us out for any kind of attention. When she was three years old, we woke up to discover that she had gotten sick in the night, grabbed a bowl from the kitchen, and threw up in it. She never even woke us. While she certainly made house management easy, I started to realize that she and I didn't have much of a connection, and I remember the quiet voice of the Holy Spirit prompting me to talk about her to a family counselor in our church. It was a humbling conversation because I felt I had failed my daughter.

The counselor was so gentle and kind. She gave me a few attachment exercises to do with Lulu to restore the attachment that we had both missed out on. The exercises were effective, but the Lord was not done restoring our relationship. He would prompt me every time I walked by Lulu to touch her hair. Just a simple, gentle stroke of her hair as I passed by on my way to change loads of laundry or pull dinner out of the oven. It wasn't easy for me. It didn't come naturally to stop a task to be affectionate. But I am so grateful that God did not give up on me. Prompt after prompt, he helped me restore a connection with my daughter. To this day, when she comes up to me, she touches my hair. When I walk by her, it's now an instinct to touch hers. I can't even imagine where we would be relationally if the Lord had never nudged me. Because of his consistent prompting, my daughter and I now have a beautiful relationship. She's still definitely independent, but she's affectionate and warm, and I am so grateful for God's never-ending grace.

The Holy Spirit has also whispered words of correction to me. When we walk by the Spirit, Galatians 5:16–17 tells us, we will not gratify the desires of the flesh. Because we are human, we are always going to be struggling with this, but when walking in relationship with the Spirit, we are aware of our need to be sanctified; therefore, we will be able to recognize the

Holy Spirit's voice of correction, because it will oppose our flesh.

I wrote a blog post on January 14, 2014, about an impactful conversation I had with God on that day. The twins were barely two years old and the other children were four, six, and eight. My plate was full. One of my biggest struggles at the time was cleaning the high chairs. The twins ate meals or snacks five times a day, which meant I cleaned ten high chairs per day. I was joking with God that I thought the devil lived in the high chairs, because every time I went to clean them, I experienced an intense amount of self-pity. It was the spot where I wallowed in thoughts of the day's endless tasks while I scrubbed crusted-up avocado out of the crevices. Right at that moment, I heard the Holy Spirit ask me, *What if these high chairs were Jesus's feet?* I went straight to the Word, finding Colossians 3:23: "Whatever you do, work heartily, as for the Lord and not for men." Later, I reread the story of Mary washing Jesus's feet and was so stirred over her affection and humility that I imagined doing the same. It was one of those moments that changed my perspective on mundane tasks in the household, and they became acts of serving my Lord. Every time I scrubbed the high chairs after that, I experienced a holy moment, imagining myself washing Jesus's feet. The high chairs became a place of worship, and I had the twins eat in them for far too long out of reluctance to get rid of them!

Life Decisions

During my senior year of high school, I became obsessed with the idea of walking in God's will. I needed to choose a college, and it was the first time I realized a decision could alter the path for my life. I knew I would probably meet my future spouse during or around the time I attended college, and the idea of setting roots in an entirely different area held significant weight. I sat with my dad after dinner one night and asked him, "Dad, I have been asking God over and over where to go, and he hasn't guided me. I do not want to make any decisions if it's out of his will for me." His response was so simple. "Sister," he said, "if you are walking with the Lord, you are in his will. Everything else will sort itself out." It wasn't the answer I was looking for, yet it took a huge weight off my shoulders. God is sovereign, and his plans for us are already set in place.

Romans 12:1–2 says,

> I appeal to you therefore, brothers, by the mercies of God, to present your bodies as a living sacrifice, holy and acceptable to God, which is your spiritual worship. Do not be conformed to this world, but be transformed by the renewal of your mind, that by testing you may discern what is the will of God, what is good and acceptable and perfect.

These verses have become important for our family, as we want our children to live lives of sacrifice to God, holy and acceptable. If they are living for God, then discernment will play a large role in their lives, so that when big decisions come, they can be led by the Spirit. And if they can't hear from the Holy Spirit about a specific direction, they will know, since they are walking with God, that "for those who love God all things work together for good, for those who are called according to his purpose" (Rom. 8:28).

I ended up meeting Jason the year after I graduated from college, just one mile from campus. The decision to attend that university ultimately led me to the love of my life, the father of my children. However, I never heard God's voice in that decision. It was a perfect testament to what my father had said and what Romans 12:1–2 says. I cannot claim I was striving for holiness during that time, but I can say that all things worked together, and I am so grateful they did! God is so good, his mercies endure forever, and his faithfulness continues through all generations.

Jason and I have had our fair share of change and uncertainty. Thankfully we can laugh about our life, because from the outside it can look quite messy. In our seventeen years of marriage, we have experienced ten moves (one across the country), multiple jobs, a few job losses, miscarriage, cancer, unexpected twins, and many more unplanned trials and experiences. There is absolutely no way we could have navigated these situations without a relationship with the Lord. We see his blessings abound and are constantly in awe of his work in our lives. We've had a number of situations that required difficult decision-making and deep faith. In some of these situations, the Holy Spirit has directed us through the Word and through prayer, and other times we've had to make a decision based on discernment. In such times, we always pray for protection. Jesus said,

My sheep hear my voice, and I know them, and they follow me. I give them eternal life, and they will never perish, and no one will snatch them out of my hand. My Father, who has given them to me, is greater than all, and no one is able to snatch them out of the Father's hand. (John 10:27–29)

We know by his words that we are protected. We have bought and sold a few homes and have put offers on dozens of others. Sometimes I would become so attached to a home, then become completely disappointed when the deal fell through. But we have learned through experience that many of those homes would not have worked out for the good of our family.

When we lived in the Bay Area of California, we searched almost two years for a home that had enough land for chickens and goats. We made offers on several different homes and always prayed for protection in case the homes were not meant for us. Not once did our offer ever get accepted. It was frustrating and heartbreaking, and we were so confused. Then the company Jason was working for got hit hard when the Great Recession came in 2008, and he ended up leaving his job to protect the owner. Had we purchased a home at the peak of the market, we would have lost a lot of money and had no income to support our mortgage.

I do not want to overspiritualize our real estate experiences, but I do profoundly believe in praying for protection in times when you step out in faith in making a decision. Psalm 91 is a beautiful chapter that describes the vast love and protection God provides. With verses such as "He who dwells in the shelter of the Most High will abide in the shadow of the Almighty. I will say to the LORD, 'My refuge and my fortress, my God, in whom I trust'" (vv. 1–2), and "He will cover you with his pinions, and under his wings you will find refuge; his faithfulness is a shield and buckler" (v. 4), we can be entirely confident in his protection and find peace in his shelter, even in making decisions on things such as our children's education or which home to buy. However, that is not to say we will not face difficulties or sorrow. It took years of my adult life to work through the understanding of suffering.

Throughout my teen and early adult years, I somehow created this notion that if someone followed Christ, then their life
would reflect their commitment to Christ through prosperity. It
took many mountains and valleys for me to finally understand
that suffering is part of our spiritual walk. I remember reading
Pilgrim's Progress with the children and finally understanding
the Christian walk. It doesn't look like monetary prosperity.
That can be an outcome, but it's not the actual fruit. The Christian walk looks like faithfulness. It looks like reliance on our
heavenly Father through high salaries or through unemployment, through health or through cancer, through new babies
or through miscarriage.

Psalm 91:11–13 says, "For he will command his angels con-
cerning you to guard you in all your ways. On their hands they
will bear you up, lest you strike your foot against a stone. You
will tread on the lion and the adder; the young lion and the
serpent you will trample underfoot." It is important to note
that God promises protection in these verses, but he does not
promise the absence of danger or risk. He does not command
the angels to remove the stone your foot strikes against nor
remove the lion and the adder. But he does promise that his
angels will bear you up. So when you are bouncing that colicky
baby or soothing your autistic child, when you are listening to
a troubling diagnosis or burying your father too early, understand that God's protection abounds. As you walk through
the Christian life, you will not always be able to make sense
of sorrow or loss, but you can always rely on the God of all
comfort—and he's trustworthy.

We teach God's promises to our children because they need
to understand that life is not always going to be easy. It is hard
for them to comprehend true sorrow or setbacks when we are

always providing for them and protecting them, but we also need to look for opportunities to teach of God's protection and comfort in their own personal relationship with God.

There Is No Junior Holy Spirit

Jason and I were upstairs in our loft bedroom getting ready for bed when our oldest son, Carter, newly turned eight, came to us in tears. He was shaken up and could barely speak. He told us he'd had the same bad dream again. Carter had been experiencing a repetitive dream for about two years that he never wanted to share. It was too frightening to talk about, so we always just sat with him and prayed with him, and would often have to lie next to him until he fell back asleep. It was a hard situation to be in as a parent because we wanted to help him so badly but it was too difficult for him to let us. That evening was different, though. We were finally able to persuade him to share the details of the dream that had deeply troubled him for so long. And Carter began describing, in great detail, the book of Revelation. Of course, he used childlike terms to describe things such as the tribes and the beast, but his recap of his dream was so parallel. Carter had never read Revelation, and we had not introduced the book to our family yet. Jason and I just kept staring at each other, wide-eyed, as our son walked us through the details, both of us thinking how terrifying it must be for a child. The worst part is that he always woke up at the same exact moment in the dream, just before Babylon's fall. Jason was able to comfort Carter, telling him he had dreamed about a book in the Bible, a very confusing and sometimes scary book, but the good news is that Christ comes and wins the battle! They went downstairs together and read Revelation 19–22 so that Carter could see for himself what happened.

While Jason was reading with Carter, I asked the Lord what on earth to do about this situation. I'll be honest, it was a little bit daunting for me, the idea of my eight-year-old child dreaming about a prophetic book in the Bible that I couldn't fully comprehend. When Jason returned to our bedroom after he'd seen Carter settled and asleep, we held hands and prayed for guidance on what had just happened. We both decided we needed to seek counsel from some parental mentors who were years ahead of us in their parenting journey. The next day, I contacted a few mentors and Jason did the same. One of my mentors used a phrase that has stuck with me ever since. When she was asking if I believed that the Holy Spirit could give people dreams and visions, I had responded, "Well, yes, it says so in the Bible." Then she said, "Well, Jodi, there is no junior Holy Spirit. It's not like children get less of what God has to offer them just because they're younger." While I still didn't understand why my son was dreaming of Revelation, I completely understood what she meant, and it changed my perspective on children and their ability to have an intimate relationship with God.

Carter's dream shook up Jason and me about our parenting. At the time, Carter and Everett were attending a Christian school, and we were comfortable with that decision. However, we both were challenged by what had happened and wondered if the Lord wanted something different for our family. I had a pressing prompt that we needed to invest more time into these precious gifts given to us. On one of my runs, I asked the Lord to guide me. I felt a nudge to pull my children from school but was terrified over the responsibility of their education as well as having to spend so much time with them. I didn't think I could homeschool. I knew I was too selfish—and I didn't mind admitting it!

That afternoon, when the three youngest were napping and the older two were still at school, I was catching up on my daily Bible reading and the day's Scripture happened to include Deuteronomy 6:4–9:

> Hear, O Israel: The LORD our God, the LORD is one. You shall love the LORD your God with all your heart and with all your soul and with all your might. And these words that I command you today shall be on your heart. You shall teach them diligently to your children, and shall talk of them when you sit in your house, and when you walk by the way, and when you lie down, and when you rise. You shall bind them as a sign on your hand, and they shall be as frontlets between your eyes. You shall write them on the doorposts of your house and on your gates.

I knew in that moment that I was being charged by the Holy Spirit to teach my children diligently. My fear of homeschooling vanished, and I knew with every fiber of my being that it was my calling.

Every fear I had about homeschooling was obliterated. The peace, beauty, and joy that permeated our home, specifically in that first year, were so evident that Jason couldn't wait to get home each day to see his family and find out what we had read about and what verses and hymns we were working on. The children were content, and I had never been so fulfilled as a wife and a mother. I understand that walking in obedience doesn't always come with such abundance, but homeschooling has been one of the most rewarding acts of obedience I have ever experienced. I am so grateful for the dream Carter encountered, because it led us to the start of a beautiful journey for our family.

To this day, Carter still has dreams about Revelation. He has a journal filled with them, and we encourage him to seek out the scriptural understanding of each dream. He has shared many of them with us, including vivid descriptions of the New Jerusalem. I haven't quite fully comprehended the purpose of him having such dreams, but I do rest confident in the words of Joel 2:28: "And it shall come to pass afterward, that I will pour out my Spirit on all flesh; your sons and your daughters shall prophesy, your old men shall dream dreams, and your young men shall see visions." I will never be able to understand the mysteries God speaks about throughout the Bible, but what I do know is that there is no such thing as a junior Holy Spirit.

CONCLUSION

Johann Wyss revealed his reason for writing *The Swiss Family Robinson* near the end of his book, and I can't help but feel the same:

> My great wish is that young people who read this record of our lives and adventures should learn from it how admirably suited is the peaceful, industrious, and pious life of a cheerful, united family to the formation of strong, pure, and manly character. None takes a better place in the great national family, none is happier or more beloved than he that goes forth from such a home to fulfill new duties, and to gather fresh interests around him.[1]

While it is a vulnerable experience to share about our family's story, I am encouraged in knowing that I do so as an act of obedience. I've known for years that I needed to write this book, yet I neglected to do so out of apathy and busyness. However, I'm confident that the Lord has made everything beautiful in its time, and so my prayer is that as you hold this book within your hands, you are encouraged, and its message is divinely applicable in your life for such a time as this.

Let's raise up honorable, industrious, cheerful children who will become healthy and whole adults who are strong in character. May the Lord bless you and keep you as you navigate through this adventurous journey of parenting!

RECIPES

Most of these recipes are easy to make, healthy, and cost-efficient. I do hope that they turn out to be delicious and fulfilling for your family. I don't typically measure or weigh ingredients for many of our meals, so they end up tasting a little different every single time, which adds some extra adventure to our time in the kitchen. Enjoy!

SNACKS

While we were purists in the first several years of Carter's healing journey, we have learned to relax significantly with some of our snacks. Now that the children are older and actively participating in work and sports, and we have a budget that allows for it, we will purchase snacks such as potato chips made with avocado oil and granola bars made with simple, whole ingredients. The important part of choosing convenience food is knowing and understanding how to read labels and pick the best options. Learning to read labels comes with time and experience, but will suit you and your children well when life becomes a little too busy to make all of your snacks from scratch. Below are some recipes of our tried-and-true snack favorites when we were eating completely clean and pure.

SPROUTED ALMONDS

Almonds are loaded with antioxidants and packed with vitamin E, magnesium, protein, and fiber. All raw nuts contain enzyme inhibitors. When they are sprouted, their full nutritional potential is unlocked as these inhibited enzymes are activated. Sprouting also makes foods easier to digest.

Raw almonds
Sea salt
Raw apple cider vinegar

Fully submerge raw almonds in water, leaving at least three inches of water on top, and let them soak overnight with 2 tbsp raw apple cider vinegar; the vinegar will jump-start the enzyme activation. Drain the almonds, submerge again with fresh water and apple cider vinegar, and soak for another 12 hours. Continue this process until you see the almonds start to sprout or crack on the ends. Rinse the almonds and then pat dry. You can toss them with salt and spread them out on paper towels for at least 24 hours or put them on cookie sheets and dehydrate them in the oven at 150° for at least 10 hours. Dehydrating in the oven will achieve a crunchy consistency (our preference), while towel drying will keep them moist and soft.

HOMEMADE POPCORN

Stovetop popcorn is probably the cheapest, most flavor-filled snack you can make. While popcorn isn't always the healthiest option for a snack, it is fun for family movie nights or for entertaining guests. Making it at home allows you to control the nutrition content and seasonings.

3 tbsp	coconut oil
1 cup	popcorn kernels (we prefer tricolor)
	salt and butter, to taste
	optional seasonings: nutritional yeast, red pepper flakes, black pepper, drizzled honey

Use a large pot with a lid. Over medium heat, add oil to pot and drop two kernels in. Have potholders ready to shimmy the hot pot. Cover the pot and wait for the kernels to pop. Once the kernels pop, drop in the remaining kernels and cover again. Shimmy the pot so they evenly disperse.

Once you start hearing the kernels pop, shimmy the pot occasionally so that the unpopped kernels will get cooked evenly. Once the popping slows down to about one pop per second, remove from heat. Add butter immediately and use a large wooden spoon to melt and disperse the butter while the pot is still hot. Transfer to a large bowl and season to taste.

BAKED AND SEASONED KALE CHIPS

Chips tend to be our family's greatest vice. They are an easy snack and fill you up quite quickly, but they're not the healthiest to have on the daily, which is why we try to add in other vegetable-based snacks. Kale chips are easy to make, nutritious, and taste delicious.

    1 bunch   kale
     1 tbsp   avocado or olive oil
      1 tsp   sea salt
              optional seasonings: garlic powder, chili flakes,
              cumin, liquid aminos

Preheat oven to 325°. Rinse and thoroughly dry kale. The kale must be fully dry before baking. Cut the leaves from the stalks (discard stalks or use for another purpose), tear into chip-size pieces, and place on a non-insulated cookie sheet so that the kale leaves make an arch shape, with room for air flow underneath. Drizzle or lightly spray kale with oil, then sprinkle with salt and any optional seasonings.

Bake until the edges brown, 15–20 minutes.

ROASTED GARBANZO BEANS

Garbanzo beans (or chickpeas) are packed with soluble fiber. They don't digest until they get to the large intestine, which is a key factor in stabilizing acid levels and overall colon health. They also are one of the only vegetables that don't lose their nutritional value when canned. The recipe below is for using canned garbanzo beans. For big families on a budget or for those looking for the added health benefits of sprouting, I suggest buying them dry in bulk, soaking them, and then following the recipes. Well-seasoned roasted garbanzo beans tend to have the same consistency as Corn Nuts but are much healthier! Below are two different options for seasonings.

» *Spicy Rosemary Beans*

2 (15 oz) cans	organic garbanzo beans
2 tsp	avocado oil
2 tbsp	chopped fresh rosemary
2 tbsp	coconut palm sugar
1 tsp	sea salt
¼ tsp	cayenne pepper

Preheat oven to 350°. Rinse and dry beans thoroughly (they will not get crunchy unless they're completely dry). Mix all ingredients together in a bowl. Make sure the seasonings are evenly distributed. Spread on a rimmed cookie sheet.

Bake for approximately 40 minutes or until they are nice and crunchy, almost burned.

» *Maple Cinnamon Beans*

2 (15 oz) cans	organic garbanzo beans
2 tsp	coconut oil
2 tbsp	coconut palm sugar
2 tsp	cinnamon
¼ tsp	sea salt

Preheat oven to 350°. Rinse and dry beans thoroughly (they will not get crunchy unless they're completely dry). Mix all ingredients together in a bowl, and spread on a rimmed cookie sheet.

Bake for approximately 40 minutes or until they are nice and crunchy, almost burned.

These are very delicious and are amazing on top of yogurt, mixed in granola, or just as a sweet snack.

You can combine both recipes and serve with aged cheese and fruit.

HOMEMADE HUMMUS

Most children will happily eat raw vegetables as long as there's something for them to dip them in. Since ranch dressing isn't always the healthiest or most cost-effective option, hummus comes in as a strong dip alternative. Not only does it taste great, but as mentioned, garbanzo beans have a lot to offer nutritionally. Homemade hummus ends up costing about one-third of the price of store-bought hummus and is much healthier, as you can choose a healthier oil than the soybean oil usually used in purchased hummus.

2 (15 oz) cans	garbanzo beans
¼ cup	tahini
¼ cup	lemon juice
4 cloves	garlic
2 tsp	sea salt
½ tsp	black pepper
1 tsp	cumin
¼ cup	olive oil
	optional toppings: smoked paprika, pine nuts, olive oil, parsley

Drain half of the liquid from the beans. Put tahini and lemon juice in a food processor or blender first. Whip for about a minute, then slowly add the remaining ingredients until you get a smooth, whipped batch of hummus. Sprinkle with optional toppings and refrigerate before serving.

BAKED SWEET POTATO FRIES

Sweet potato fries are one of our favorite savory sides or comforting snacks. Sweet potatoes are incredibly filling, provide many antioxidants, are rich in beta-carotene, and are a great source of fiber, vitamins, and minerals. When the fries are adequately seasoned, most children, even those who are used to a more Western diet, will never refuse them. I tend to make these when we have company with smaller children.

6–10 med/lg	sweet potatoes
¼ cup	cornstarch
6 tbsp	avocado oil
2 tsp	sea salt
	optional spices: garlic powder, parsley, ground black pepper to taste

Wash and slice sweet potatoes into very slim, fry-shaped pieces. I leave the skin on for added nutrition. Mix remaining ingredients in a bowl and then add the fries to the bowl, tossing for adequate coverage.

Preheat oven to 425° and lay fries in a single layer on oiled or parchment paper–covered cookie sheets. Bake for 20 minutes, flip them over, and bake for another 15–20 minutes. Fries will look crispy and puffy when done. Sprinkle with optional spices and additional salt to taste.

RAW CACAO BALLS

I absolutely love chocolate, and it tends to be an incessant need of mine after dinner. Unfortunately, most commercial chocolate is filled with ingredients that are less than ideal. This recipe is packed with antioxidants, healthy medium chain fats, protein, fiber, and omega 3s. Once you understand the ratio of coconut oil to solids, you can get creative with other ingredients by adding your favorite crushed nuts, nut butters, or various seeds.

2 cups	raw shredded coconut
¾ cup	maple syrup
¾ cup	cacao powder
1 tsp	vanilla extract
1 tsp	cinnamon
⅓ cup	coconut oil (in liquid form)
⅓ cup	raw almond butter
⅓ cup	dark chocolate chips
⅓ cup	chia seeds (pre-activated by soaking in ⅓ cup water for at least 10 minutes or overnight to achieve extra enzymes)
dash	sea salt

Mix all ingredients together, then use a teaspoon to dollop the batter into small balls on a cookie sheet. Set in the freezer. The batter should harden within ten minutes, and then they're ready to eat. These cacao balls do best if kept cold.

FERMENTS

Experimenting with kombucha and water kefir is an excellent science project for the family! Many times ferments vary due to the temperature, duration, and flavors or seasonings you add. Part of the excitement of ferments is experiencing the different variation in flavors every week. In our current season of life, we rely on buying our kombucha and water kefir drinks from the store, but I will include our most reliable sauerkraut recipe, because it is easy and always provides a fantastic, gut-supporting topping to put on nearly everything from eggs to chili, nachos, and salad.

SAUERKRAUT

Filled with beneficial lactic acid bacteria, a major aid in digestive health, sauerkraut is a traditional fermented food that is a staple in our kitchen. The fermentation process turns the natural carbohydrates of the cabbage into lactic acid, which then works with all of the healthy bacteria in your gut to reproduce healthy bacteria, creating a natural cleanse of toxins in your body.

3 med	heads cabbage (green or red)
3 tbsp	sea salt (Real Salt or a blend of mineral-rich salts)
1 cup	filtered water
	optional spices: cumin, turmeric, garlic, pepper, mustard seed

Shred cabbage, then add salt and any optional spices. Beat with a wooden spoon or tenderizer until the combination is juicy. The more juice, the more room it has to work during the fermentation process.

Add water. Mix. If you have a previous batch of sauerkraut (homemade or store-bought), add the remaining juice from that batch to this batch. This will further benefit the bacteria reproduction process—similar to making yogurt or sourdough.

Fill clean glass jars of any size (wide mouth jars are easiest to use). Pack the mixture down and leave about one inch of room for the fermentation process to work. Make sure the cabbage is fully submerged in liquid, or the top layer of cabbage may mold. You can use a cabbage leaf to cover the top of the cabbage and place a glass weight or thoroughly cleaned rock on it to help keep the cabbage submerged. Cover each jar loosely with an airtight lid.

Leave jars on a shelf for 5–14 days (the longer the duration, the stronger the ferment) in an area where the temperature remains mild (anywhere from 68–76°) and out of direct light. After about 3–4 days, "burp the jars," which means to release the lids to let the air out, then set the lids back on, not tightening entirely. By the end of the ferment, you should be able to see and hear the sauerkraut fizzing and bubbling, which is proof that it's living and active.

When your kraut is fermented to your taste, remove the cabbage leaf and weight. If you find a bit of scum at the top, know that this is not bad; it's just not attractive, and you can skim it off. Tighten the lid fully and put the jars into the refrigerator. The longer they're in the fridge, the better they taste; however, they are ready to consume at this point.

» *Optional Vegetables*

You can add any extra vegetables or herbs to your sauerkraut. This is a recipe that can use older, wilted veggies and still maximize their health benefits. Since it will be chopped and fermented, the condition of the veggie doesn't really matter as long as it is not moldy. Thinly chopped radishes, Swiss chard, carrots, and other types of root vegetables work well as additional textures and flavors in the sauerkraut.

LACTO-FERMENTED ZUCCHINI

Cabbage is not the only vegetable you can ferment. In fact, most vegetables can be fermented, although those with the highest water content ferment best. Like sauerkraut, lacto-fermented vegetables contain beneficial lactic acid bacteria. They are rich in vitamins C and B, contain antioxidants and minerals, and help keep a healthy gut. One of our favorite ferments, aside from sauerkraut, is zucchini.

4 med	firm zucchini (make sure there are no soft spots)
8 cups	filtered water
6 tbsp	sea salt
6 cloves	garlic, peeled
2 sprigs	dill (optional)

This recipe should provide at least 2 quarts of fermented zucchini. Place a sprig of dill, if desired, in each of 2 clean 1 quart wide mouth mason jars. Rinse and cut zucchini into rounds or sticks, and divide equally into canning jars with the garlic. Create a brine by mixing the water and sea salt. Cover zucchini with the brine, leaving an inch of headspace at the top of each jar and pushing the zucchini as far down as possible so the brine can submerge them.

Like the sauerkraut, weigh down the zucchini using a cabbage leaf and clean rock or glass weight to ensure the brine stays above the zucchini. Cover loosely with the jar lid.

Leave on a shelf out of direct light for 7–14 days, burping the jars at least once in that duration. Remove weight, skim any scum, and place the lids on tightly. Store in the refrigerator for up to six weeks. The liquid will be cloudy and the zucchini should taste sour and tangy.

STOCKS

BONE BROTH

Bone broth has received some major recognition in the past few years, and for good reason. When you use healthy bones from grass-fed beef or free-range chicken to make stock, you receive numerous benefits and health support from natural collagen, glutamine, amino acids, calcium, magnesium, sulfur, and much more. Drinking bone broth will improve gut health, bone mass, and joint support and even tighten your skin. Bone broth can and should be used as a base for many recipes, a sipping snack, or as a stock for soups. You cannot really do bone broth wrong, as any vegetables and herbs can be used, but our simple recipe is below.

1	chicken carcass, or beef bones from 1–2 meals
1	onion, quartered, any kind
1 stalk	celery, roughly chopped (no need to cut the top off)
4–6 cloves	garlic
2 tbsp	sea salt

Combine all ingredients in a stockpot or slow cooker, and fill with filtered water. Place the lid on and bring to a boil, then simmer on low for 24 hours or more. Remove all the bones and vegetables and strain the remaining stock into wide mouth quart size mason jars. Refrigerate or freeze. If you plan on freezing, be sure to leave at least 3 inches headspace for the broth to expand.

VEGETABLE BROTH

There were many times when I needed broth for a recipe but didn't have any frozen bones stored. Vegetable broth may not provide as much rich collagen or as many minerals as bone broth, but it is still healthier and cheaper than anything bought in the store. I typically do not use my best vegetables for broth but hold on to and freeze the ends and pieces of veggies I have used in main dishes. This includes the unwanted parts of any vegetables, as long as they are not moldy. Making broth is also an excellent opportunity to clean out your veggie drawer. There are four necessities for vegetable broth: onions (any kind), celery, carrots, and sea salt. As long as those four ingredients are included, any and all other vegetables and spices can be added for extra taste and nutrition.

    1–2 onions, quartered
    3+ ribs celery or celery tops/bottoms
    3 carrots, cut into 2–3 inch pieces
    salt to taste
      filtered water

Optional:
    5–8   cloves garlic
  2 tbsp olive oil
        lemon
        pepper to taste
        vegetable ends and pieces
        bay leaves to taste
        thyme to taste

Place onions, carrots, celery, and any other vegetables in a stockpot or slow cooker, and fill with filtered water. Season to taste. Place the lid on and bring to a boil, then reduce heat to low, partially covering the pot so nutrients and flavors stay in the broth. Simmer for at least forty-five minutes. Strain and store broth in wide mouth quart size mason jars. If you plan on freezing, be sure to leave at least 3 inches headspace for the broth to expand.

MEALS

I am not the most creative person in the kitchen, nor am I an excellent cook. However, I do appreciate feeding my family healthy food in the most economical way possible, and we have some tried-and-true staples that have proven themselves healthy, tasty, and cost-efficient. The recipes I share below are made at least once a week and have been used for many years. We have yet to tire of them, and they have always provided nourishment. I tend to throw things together by instinct, but I will provide the most accurate recipes possible. You will most likely want to play with ratios to best satisfy your taste and consistency preferences.

POWER PANCAKES

Filled with protein and fiber, these are heavy enough to hold the hungriest of kids over until lunchtime! These are not your typical fluffy white pancakes. They are dense and hearty and have a bit of a muffin texture. This recipe makes a big batch, enough for a large meal plus extras to freeze and toast for breakfast on the run—or use as bread for almond butter sandwiches, a favorite in our household!

1 cup	rolled oats or ½ cup steel cut oats
1 cup	chia seeds

*Optional: soak oats and seeds in 4 cups water with 2 tsp apple cider vinegar for 8–24 hours beforehand to activate enzymes and lower phytic acid. Drain the oats and seeds prior to mixing with the following ingredients.

4 cups	GF all-purpose flour
2 cups	almond flour
8	eggs
¼ cup	molasses
¼ cup	coconut palm sugar
1 tsp	baking soda
2 cups	milk (any kind; we use raw or whole fat coconut)
2 tsp	cinnamon
2 tbsp	vanilla extract

Mix all ingredients together. It should be very thick, almost like a muffin batter, but runny enough to pour. Add more milk or flour to adjust thickness, if needed. This will not alter the taste.

Preheat a griddle over medium heat, and grease the pan with some coconut oil. Almond flour can burn easily, so keeping the griddle well-oiled will avoid burning. These power pancakes cook and look differently than standard pancakes. They require a slow, low cook and even a few pats with the spatula to make sure they cook all the way through.

Once you understand the ratio of flours and liquids, you can add fruit, pumpkin purée, and different seeds. Top with maple syrup or raw honey and enjoy!

EVERYTHING BUT THE SINK QUICK CHILI

Summer or winter, this is a weekly staple in our home. The vegetables, spices, and grains may change each time, but the comfort of rich broth and savory flavors remains the same. While it's healthier to make this soup with sprouted beans and rice and fresh vegetables, I am going to give you the quick and easy version here for those last-minute meals. (Follow the phase 1 directions of the Garden Enchilada Pie recipe below for the sprouting version.)

1 lb	grass-fed ground beef or ground turkey
1	yellow onion, diced
2 tsp	chili powder
3 cloves	garlic, crushed
2 tsp	sea salt
½ tsp	crushed red chili pepper
2	bell peppers, red, yellow, or orange, chopped
1 (10–12 oz) bag	frozen organic chopped spinach or kale, or 3 cups fresh spinach/kale/Swiss chard
1½ cups	wild rice

2 (15 oz) cans	organic black beans
1 (15 oz) can	organic kidney beans
48 oz	homemade or store-bought bone broth
2 cups	green enchilada sauce or salsa
8 oz	frozen organic corn
1 bunch	fresh cilantro, chopped

Brown the ground meat and onion together with seasonings in a stockpot. Add broth and sauce or salsa when meat is fully cooked. Add bell peppers and greens. Rinse rice and drain and rinse beans, then add to the pot. Simmer for 30–40 minutes. Season to taste. When rice is fully cooked, add cilantro and corn. Heat through. Serve with sour cream, diced avocado, fresh chopped cabbage, fresh chopped red onion, and sliced olives.

GARDEN ENCHILADA PIE

A one-pan meal filled with sprouted beans, sprouted rice, and seasonal vegetables. Flavored with Mexican seasonings and topped with cheese, this meal is a digestive-friendly family favorite.

This meal can be made in two phases. The first phase is sprouting the beans and rice and cooking them. If you're in a hurry, bypass this step entirely by using 2–3 cans of organic black beans and one package of organic precooked rice.

» **Phase 1**

1 cup	brown or wild rice
3 cups	dried black beans

¼ cup   acid medium (apple cider vinegar, yogurt, or kefir)

12 cups   bone broth, store-bought stock, or water with salt to taste

Rinse beans and rice and put in a large glass or enamel bowl. Add purified water to cover by about 2 inches. Add acid medium and cover bowl with a breathable cloth for 2–3 days. Check every day to make sure the water still fully covers the beans, and add more water if needed. The beans will be officially "sprouted" when you see little tails popping out.

The process of sprouting adds vitamin C to your beans and grains. It also neutralizes phytic acid (which allows the nutritional benefits of the beans/grain to be absorbed into the body), increases the amount of vitamin B, and produces special enzymes for easy digestion.

In the morning, rinse and drain beans and rice, pour them into a stockpot or slow cooker with liquid of choice (bone broth, stock, or water with salt), and simmer on low from morning until Phase 2, making sure there's enough liquid throughout the day.

» **Phase 2**

1 lb   grass-fed ground beef or ground turkey

1   yellow onion, chopped

2 tbsp   chili powder

1 tsp   garlic powder

1 tsp   cumin

1 tsp   sea salt

½ tsp   crushed red pepper

prepared rice and beans

3 cups   finely chopped dark green seasonal veggies (spinach, Swiss chard, cabbage, or zucchini)

12   corn tortillas

16 oz   organic green enchilada sauce (add a few
ounces of coconut milk if too spicy, or replace
with 8 oz salsa and 8 oz broth)
2 cups   shredded cheese (raw or Mexican)
2 (5 oz) cans   sliced olives

Preheat oven to 425° and butter or oil a 10x15 pan or Pyrex dish.

Brown onion with ground meat and all seasonings until meat is fully cooked. To assemble, lay 6 corn tortillas in the pan. You will likely need to tear some of them to cover the bottom entirely. Spread evenly with beans and rice, then meat mixture, then fresh vegetables. Top with remaining 6 tortillas (tear accordingly). Pour enchilada sauce over tortillas evenly, letting it soak down at the bottom. Sprinkle with cheese and top with olives. Cook uncovered for 30 minutes or until cheese has melted, vegetables are cooked down, and tortilla edges are browned.

MOSTLY VEGGIE MEATLOAF

Packed with veggies, fiber, and flavor, this meatloaf is a household favorite. We typically roast sweet potatoes and carrots on a cookie sheet for our side dish as it bakes, and often will serve a meatloaf square over raw spinach.

1 cup   rolled oats
¼ cup   flax seeds

*Optional: soak oats and seeds in 2 cups of water with 1 tsp of apple cider vinegar 8–24 hours before making to activate enzymes and lower phytic acid. Drain the oats and seeds prior to mixing with the following ingredients.

2 lbs	lean ground turkey or grass-fed beef (or 1 lb each)
¼ cup	sulfate-free Dijon mustard
1 cup	raw cheese (mozzarella or feta work as well)
2 tsp	white pepper
2	eggs
1 cup	GF bread crumbs
2 tsp	minced rosemary, fresh or dried
1 bunch	green onions, chopped
2	zucchini, shredded, or 1 bag (12–18 oz) organic broccoli slaw
3 cloves	fresh garlic, minced
2 tsp	sea salt

Combine all ingredients and divide in half. Form two loaves and place in a 9x13 pan, leaving space not only around the edges of the pan but also between the loaves. This will keep them from drying out. Bake uncovered at 350° for at least 45 minutes, then test temperature with a meat thermometer. Once it reaches 160°, remove from the oven and let rest a few minutes before slicing. You can also form the ingredients into burgers and grill them or fry them in a pan.

NOTES

Introduction

1. "4 Kids/Home Birth—Jim Gaffigan," YouTube video, 4:26, uploaded by jimgaffigan, April 16, 2020, https://www.youtube.com/watch?v=-Jf2IGylAhE.

Chapter 1 Awareness

1. Don and Katie Fortune, *Discover Your Children's Gifts* (Grand Rapids: Chosen, 1989), 72.

2. Frank Gilbreth Sr., "Motion Study as an Increase of National Wealth," *The Annals of the American Academy of Political and Social Science* 59 (1915): 96.

3. Gary Chapman and Ross Campbell, *The 5 Love Languages of Children* (Chicago: Northfield Publishing, 2012), 22.

Chapter 2 Communication

1. "2005 Nov 03—E. Mark Cummings—Children and Marital Conflict," YouTube video, 1:08:51, uploaded by Helmke Library, September 16, 2019, https://www.youtube.com/watch?v=aFdjcUxe7FI.

2. R. T. Kendall Ministries, "The Friday Night School of Theology: The Blood of Jesus," accessed April 6, 2021, https://rtkendallministries.com/wp-content/uploads/KT-11-The-Blood-of-Jesus.pdf.

3. Kristen Jensen, *Good Pictures Bad Pictures: Porn-Proofing Today's Young Kids*, second edition (Richland, WA: Glen Cove Press, 2018).

4. Allison Baxter, "How Pornography Harms Children: The Advocate's Role," American Bar Association, May 1, 2014, https://www.americanbar .org/groups/public_interest/child_law/resources/child_law_practiceonline

/child_law_practice/vol-33/may-2014/how-pornography-harms-children--the
-advocate-s-role/.

5. Baxter, "How Pornography Harms Children."

6. Jensen, *Good Pictures Bad Pictures*, chapter 7.

Chapter 3 Nature

1. Paul Switzer and Wayne Ott, "Derivation of an Indoor Air Averaging Time Model from the Mass Balance Equation for the Case of Independent Source Inputs and Fixed Air Exchange Rates," *Journal of Exposure Analysis and Environmental Epidemiology* 2, suppl. 2 (1992): 113, https://www.researchgate.net/publication/236470502_Derivation_of_an_indoor_air_averaging_time_model_from_the_mass_balance_equation_for_the_case_of_independent_source_inputs_and_fixed_air_exchange_rates.

2. Yoshifumi Miyazaki et al., "Nihon Eiseigaku Zasshi (Preventive Medical Effects of Nature Therapy)," *Japanese Journal of Hygiene* 66, no. 4 (2011): 651–56, https://pubmed.ncbi.nlm.nih.gov/21996763/; Qing Li, "Effect of Forest Bathing Trips on Human Immune Function," *Environmental Health and Preventative Medicine* 15, no. 1 (2010): 9–17, https://www.ncbi.nlm.nih.gov/pmc/articles/PMC2793341/.

Chapter 4 Simplicity

1. Cindy Rollins, *Mere Motherhood: Morning Times, Nursery Rhymes, and My Journey Toward Sanctification* (Concord, NC: CiRCE Institute, 2016).

2. Stanford University, "A Clean, Well-Lighted Place," *BeWell News*, accessed May 18, 2021, https://bewell.stanford.edu/a-clean-well-lighted-place/.

3. Traci Pedersen, "Too Many Extracurricular Activities for Kids May Do More Harm Than Good," Psych Central, May 15, 2018, https://psychcentral.com/news/2018/05/15/too-many-extracurricular-activities-for-kids-may-do-more-harm-than-good#1.

4. Bill Pennington, "Doctors See a Big Rise in Injuries for Young Athletes," *New York Times*, February 22, 2005, https://www.nytimes.com/2005/02/22/sports/othersports/doctors-see-a-big-rise-ininjuries-for-young-athletes.html.

5. Julianna W. Miner, "Why 70 Percent of Kids Quit Sports by the Age 13," *Washington Post*, June 1, 2016, https://www.washingtonpost.com/news/parenting/wp/2016/06/01/why-70-percent-of-kids-quit-sports-by-age-13/.

Chapter 5 Food

1. Kelli Miller, "Can What You Eat Affect Your Mental Health?" WebMD, August 20, 2015, https://www.webmd.com/mental-health/news/20150820/food-mental-health#2.

2. Miller, "Can What You Eat Affect Your Mental Health?"

3. Sana Qadar, David Perlmutter, and James Greenblatt, "The Second Brain," *All in the Mind with Sana Qadar*, August 16, 2015, https://www.abc.net.au/radionational/programs/allinthemind/the-second-brain/6689202.

4. Sana Qadar, Perlmutter, and Greenblatt, "The Second Brain." https://pubmed.ncbi.nlm.nih.gov/24709485/.

5. Jennifer Warner, "Baby Boomers May Outlive Their Kids: High Obesity Rates Set Younger Generation Up for Poor Health, WebMD, April 9, 2010, https://www.webmd.com/children/news/20100409/baby-boomers-may-outlive-their-kids.

Chapter 6 Fitness

1. Johann David Wyss, *The Swiss Family Robinson*, Townsend Library ed. (West Berlin, NJ: Townsend Press, 2006), 148.

2. Angela Duckworth, *Grit: The Power of Passion and Perseverance* (New York: Simon and Schuster, 2018), 36.

3. Janice Thompson et al., "Physically Active Families—De-Bunking the Myth? A Qualitative Study of Family Participation in Physical Activity," *Child: Care, Health, and Development* 36, no. 2 (2010): 265–74, https://pubmed.ncbi.nlm.nih.gov/20047594/.

4. Carol Dweck, "The Power of Believing That You Can Improve," TED Talk (TEDxNorrkoping, 2014), accessed May 25, 2021, https://www.ted.com/talks/carol_dweck_the_power_of_believing_that_you_can_improve.

5. Open University, "7. Do Active Parents Have Active Children?" Open Learn, accessed May 25, 2021, https://www.open.edu/openlearn/health-sports-psychology/physical-activity-family-affair/content-section-7.

Chapter 7 Health and Wellness

1. Lauren Deville, "Oil Pulling for Oral Health," Dr. Lauren Deville, accessed May 23, 2021, https://www.drlaurendeville.com/articles/oil-pulling-oral-health/; Vagish Kumar L. Shanbhag, "Oil Pulling for Maintaining Oral Hygiene—A Review," *Journal of Traditional and Complementary Medicine* 7, no. 1 (2016): 106–9, https://www.ncbi.nlm.nih.gov/pmc/articles/PMC5198813/.

2. Ruthann Richter, "Among Teens, Sleep Deprivation an Epidemic," Stanford Medicine News Center, October 8, 2015, https://med.stanford.edu/news/all-news/2015/10/among-teens-sleep-deprivation-an-epidemic.html.

3. Michael J. Breus, "The Effects of Cortisol on Your Sleep," *Psychology Today*, April 10, 2020, https://www.psychologytoday.com/us/blog/sleep-newzzz/202004/the-effects-cortisol-your-sleep.

4. Julia Calderone, "Sleep-Deprived Kids Have Increased Diabetes Risk," *Consumer Reports*, August 15, 2017, https://www.consumerreports.org/sleeping/kids-sleeping-habits-and-type-2-diabetes-risk/.

5. Markham Heid, "What's the Best Time to Sleep? You Asked," *TIME*, April 27, 2017, https://time.com/3183183/best-time-to-sleep/.

6. Tim Newman, "What Are the Benefits of Garlic?" *Medical News Today*, August 18, 2017, https://www.medicalnewstoday.com/articles/265853#benefits.

7. Jo, "Garlic Oil for Ear Infections: Why You Should Make Your Own," *Nourishing Time* (blog), October 8, 2013, https://nourishingtime.com/garlic-oil-for-ear-infections-why-you-should-make-your-own/.

8. Keri Sutton, "Benefits of Colloidal Silver," KARE Health & Wellness, June 16, 2017, https://integrativehealthcarespringfieldmo.com/benefits-of-colloidal-silver-homeopathic-medicine-springfield-mo/.

9. Healthwise Staff, "Tea Tree Oil (Melaleuca Alternifolia)," University of Michigan Health, accessed June 5, 2021, https://www.uofmhealth.org/health-library/tn2873spec.

10. Josh Williams and M. Curtis Hobson, "Grapefruit Seed Extract," Active Health Chiropractic, accessed June 5, 2021, https://www.activehealthchiropracticstg.com/single-post/2017/05/26/grapefruit-seed-extract.

11. Dónal P. O'Mathúna, "Grapefruit Seed Extract as an Antimicrobial Agent," Relias Media, July 1, 2009, https://www.reliasmedia.com/articles/113659-grapefruit-seed-extract-as-an-antimicrobial-agent.

12. Peggy Pletcher, "9 Unexpected Benefits of Eucalyptus Oil," Healthline, July 25, 2017, https://www.healthline.com/health/9-ways-eucalyptus-oil-can-help#breathing.

13. Divya Jacob, "20 Benefits of Drinking Apple Cider Vinegar," Medicine Net, accessed June 5, 2021, https://www.medicinenet.com/20_benefits_of_drinking_apple_cider_vinegar/article.htm.

14. Cathy Wong, "The Health Benefits of Propolis," Verywell Health, accessed June 6, 2021, https://www.verywellhealth.com/propolis-what-should-i-know-about-it-88313.

15. "Elderberry Benefits," Herb Wisdom, accessed June 6, 2021, https://www.herbwisdom.com/herb-elderberry.html.

16. Amanda Barrell, "Health Benefits of Elderberry," Medical News Today, October 9, 2018, https://www.medicalnewstoday.com/articles/323288#health-benefits.

17. Chad Hagy, "5 Facts about Goldenseal Extract," Everyday Health, accessed June 6, 2021, https://www.everydayhealth.com/diet-nutrition/5-facts-about-goldenseal-extract.

18. "Epsom Salt Uses and Benefits," Salt Works, accessed June 6, 2021, https://seasalt.com/epsom-salt-uses-and-benefits.

19. Emily Cronkleton, "What Are the Benefits of a Baking Soda Bath, How Do You Take One, and Is It Safe?" Healthline, September 18, 2018, https://www.healthline.com/health/baking-soda-bath#purpose.

20. Barbie Cervoni, "What Is Calendula?" Verywell Health, June 14, 2020, https://www.verywellhealth.com/health-benefits-of-calendula-4582641.

21. Centers for Disease Control and Prevention, "New CDC Data Show Large Percentage of Antibiotics Misused in Outpatient Settings," press release, May 3, 2016, https://www.cdc.gov/media/releases/2016/p0503-unnecessary -prescriptions.html.

22. Shutterstock.com, "Effective Home Remedies to Treat Diaper Rashes," Times of India, accessed June 6, 2021, https://timesofindia.indiatimes.com /life-style/parenting/first-year/effective-home-remedies-to-treat-diaper-rashes /photostory/68936696.cms.

23. Adrian White, "Using Essential Oils for Burns," Healthline, November 2, 2018, https://www.healthline.com/health/essential-oil-for-burns.

24. Cathy Wong, "What Is Arnica?" Verywell Health, August 14, 2021, https://www.verywellhealth.com/the-benefits-of-arnica-89542.

25. G. Vighi et al., "Allergy and the Gastrointestinal System," *Clinical and Experimental Immunology* 153, suppl. 1 (2008): 3–6, https://www.ncbi.nlm .nih.gov/pmc/articles/PMC2515351/.

26. Elaine Hsiao and Thomas Fung, "Study Shows How Serotonin and a Popular Anti-Depressant Affect the Gut's Microbiota," Science Daily, September 6, 2019, https://www.sciencedaily.com/releases/2019/09/190906092809 .htm.

27. Henry Ford Health System Staff, "Antibiotics and Probiotics: Medications Affect Your Gut," *Henry Ford Live Well* (blog), June 29, 2020, https:// www.henryford.com/blog/2020/06/antibiotics-and-probiotics-how-medications -affect-your-gut.

28. WebMD, "What Is Candidiasis?" WebMD, accessed September 27, 2021, https://www.webmd.com/skin-problems-and-treatments/guide/what -is-candidiasis-yeast-infection.

29. Centers for Disease Control and Prevention, "New CDC Data Show Large Percentage of Antibiotics Misused in Outpatient Settings."

30. Catharine Paddock, "Bouts of Fever Make Us More Resilient to Cancer," Medical News Today, August 21, 2018, https://www.medicalnewstoday .com/articles/322831#The-febrile-system.

31. Silke Schmidt, "Fevers Can Have Some Cool Benefits," Science News for Students, March 20, 2019, https://www.sciencenewsforstudents.org/article /fever-can-help-immune-cells-attack.

32. Laura Markham, "What Every User of Acetaminophen Needs to Know," *Wellness* (blog), March 29, 2018, https://www.wellness.com/blog /20034/what-every-user-of-acetaminophen-needs-to-know/dr-laura-mark ham.

33. "Tylenol No Longer Deemed a Pain Reliever for Babies and Toddlers," New Beginnings, March 25, 2015, http://www.newbeginningsbirthcenter.com /tylenol-no-longer-deemed-a-pain-reliever-for-babies-and-toddlers/.

34. Baylor College of Medicine, "Understanding Acetaminophen Poisoning," Science Daily, October 11, 2002, https://www.sciencedaily.com/releases /2002/10/021014072451.htm.

Chapter 8 Biblically Grounded

1. Edward Mote, "My Hope Is Built on Nothing Less," (1834), public domain.

2. Elsie Egermeier, *Egermeier's Bible Story Book*, rev. ed., edited by Arlene Hall and illustrated by Clive Upton (Anderson, IN: Warner Press, 2007).

3. Wikipedia, s.v. "Horatio Spafford," accessed December 27, 2021, https://en.wikipedia.org/wiki/Horatio_Spafford.

4. Horatio Gates Spafford, "It Is Well with My Soul," (1873), public domain.

Chapter 9 Service

1. Jackie Hill Perry, Twitter post, July 10, 2020, https://twitter.com/jackiehillperry/status/1281582247599050753.

2. Simply Charlotte Mason, "Your Business Math Series," accessed November 12, 2021, https://simplycharlottemason.com/store/your-business-math-sports-store-edition/.

3. R. C. Sproul, "What Does the Bible Say about Christian Tithing?" Ligonier Ministries, accessed January 3, 2022, https://www.ligonier.org/learn/articles/stewardship-tithing-and-giving.

Conclusion

1. Wyss, *Swiss Family Robinson*, 423–24.

CONNECT WITH JODI

JodiMockabee.com

JODI MOCKABEE is a photographer, writer, blogger, speaker, and homeschooling mother of five living in the Black Hills of South Dakota. With a passion for health, wellness, parenting, and homemaking, Jodi blogs her family's journey and shares tips for a healthy and active lifestyle. She also writes curriculum for creative and artistic learning in a homeschool environment.

[Instagram icon] JodiMockabee

www.ingramcontent.com/pod-product-compliance
Lightning Source LLC
Chambersburg PA
CBHW060753100426
42813CB00004B/794